POWER OF YOU

D1572497

Compiled by Seema Giri
#1 International Best Selling
& Award-Winning Author

Power of You

ISBN 978-1-7350255-5-1 (hardcover)
ISBN 978-1-7350255-4-4 (paperback)

CONTENTS

INTRODUCTION

Dear Reader,

Thank you for leaning in to this powerful anthology. I was encouraged to bring *Power of You: Courage to Thrive in Uncertain Times* book forward because my desire is to help people course-correct with wisdom and experience of people who have gone through the similar situation as quickly as possible with the current global climate.

This was proven to me by the success of the last four books that became #1 International Best Sellers:
Break Free to Stand in Your Power
Break Free to Peace, Love and Unity
Break Free to Health and Vitality and
The Art of Leadership: Leading Confidently in Any Season

It is my honor and pleasure to bring forth to you amazing heart-centered authors who have opened up their hearts to you. *Power of You* is an excellent and powerful resource for you to help you break free from your challenges or barriers holding you back from becoming the leader that you are.

Each one of us needs encouragement and wisdom from someone who has walked in similar shoes before. There are some lessons that we need to learn ourselves yet there are many lessons we can learn from others and save ourselves time and pain. I hope you find lessons you can learn from the lives of these co-authors.

This book is one to be read as the spirit moves you. What do you need to hear today? Do you need a story of courage, of pathos, of redemption? Choose a chapter and see what unfolds. You will find just what you need in the pages of this book.

It is divided into three sections:

Break Free to Brighter Side: here the co-authors share the ways you can be a dynamic leader and look at the glass full even in the most difficult situations.

Step Into Your Power and Transform: here the co-authors share how you can discover your inner power to take the right actions to create the life of your design.

Own Your Greatness No Matter What: here is where the co-authors share how you can embrace your true talents unapologetically.

The following are some tips and suggestions on how to get the most out of this book and experience transformation:

1. You will need your favorite journal, favorite pen, and a quiet place where you won't get disturbed.
2. In your journal, you want to capture your current state: your fears, frustrations, and where you feel you are holding yourself back or being held back. Be as detailed as you can. This is for your eyes only.
3. First read through *all* the chapters.
4. Go to the chapter you resonated with the most and follow the tips given in that chapter. Use your journal to capture your thoughts and feelings.
5. Go to the second chapter that you resonated with and follow the tips given in that chapter. Continue doing so with the other chapters until you feel complete.

6. Review your journal. Go back over the pages, and you will gain new awareness and a new perspective of your challenges. You will notice your strengths. Perhaps you will even notice a pattern. Once you have this new insight, you will know exactly where you need to make some changes or adjustments to your life. Most importantly, you will see how far you have come in your healing journey.

As you go through this process, you will realize, as you move through your healing journey, you will resonate with the different authors' stories and tips.

Don't forget to celebrate your small wins along with the big wins!

I believe that life is supposed to be joyous and vibrant. The journey can be made with ease and grace. You're a diamond waiting to be polished so that you can shine with the gift(s) you were given in this world. In other words, you can give meaning and purpose to your challenges so that you can live your dreams.

The best way I have been able to serve is by providing creative solutions to help people grow and thrive. Compiling stories of remarkable people who have overcome some of life's most difficult challenges and thriving is one of the ways. One story at a time, one book at a time.

Now it's your turn; will you lean in to take in all that you can to change the trajectory of your life from the wisdom that you gain from these pages?

About Seema

Seema Giri is a #1 international best-selling and award-winning author, international speaker, empowerment leader, and multi-author book expert. Over the last 20 years, **she has helped more than 100,000 spiritually aligned entrepreneurs and leaders expand their consciousness, tap into**

their inner power, and unleash their true potential so that they become unstoppable in business and life. Drawing from her own experiences with chronic illness, isolation, and deep feelings of emptiness and defeat, Seema offers insight and hope to leaders who want to shine.

After years of honing her craft and sharing her own story, her latest endeavor is to help others come out of the shadows by telling their own stories. She helps leaders and entrepreneurs expand their influence and impact through her Shine Your Brilliance as an Author program and storytelling platform. **Her clients write high-impact books—sharing wisdom they gained from life-altering experiences. As they do, the lives of readers are transformed, making a massive positive impact in the world.**

Her expertise comes from a vast storehouse of experiences and opportunities including traveling around the world. She draws from 20 years of project management, coaching, and leadership experience. In addition to her own book projects and speaking engagements, she is proud to have co-authored the book **The Authorities, with New York Times Bestselling authors Dr. John Gray (***Men Are From Mars, Women Are From Venus***), Marci Shimoff (***Happiness for No Reason***), and Raymond Aaron (***Double Your Income Doing What You Love***).** In it, she chronicles her transformation from being bedridden and in chronic pain to becoming a successful entrepreneur, mother and wife. The rare combination of her personal testimony and her extensive expertise makes her a skilled and hopeful guide to all who want to tell their own stories and impact the world.

Section 1:
BREAK FREE TO BRIGHTER SIDE

LETTING GO OF THE PRESSURE MYTH
BY ARLISS DUDLEY-CASH MA, MBA

"I work better under pressure."

Have you ever said that? Have you ever heard that? I hear these five words all the time from new coaching clients. It just isn't true. It's a myth! And yet, so many people subscribe to this myth and pile on the pressure thinking they will achieve greater and greater success in their life when they actually end up overwhelmed and overworked. Procrastination, over-booking ourselves, and leaving important things to the very last minute result in feelings of overwhelm, stress, and doing less than our best. In truth, science says that our brains actually perform much worse under pressure, stress and overwhelm. Let's dive into how to identify when we are putting ourselves under pressure and how to step away from pressure as a means of negative motivation.

My Story

I used to be a huge subscriber to the Pressure Myth. When I was in high school, college and graduate school, I was a champion stresser, overbooker and procrastinator. While earning my undergraduate degree, I waited until the last 48 hours to study for my multivariable calculus final exam. I barely passed the test by a hair's breadth and it was a terrible experience. I did not learn my lesson. Later, I took 32 credits in a quarter and participated in extracurricular experiences. It was way too much. I was constantly falling behind, feeling stressed and overwhelmed. My grades deteriorated and I don't think I actually learned anything. I didn't learn my lesson. This behavior followed me into graduate school and just got worse. In graduate school, I worked 90 hours a week in the lab and took classes and played on three slow-pitch softball teams and attended football games on the weekends. Then, I got really sick. It was like my body was saying, "OK *lady, enough is enough! Cut it out!*"

On a fall day in 2012, after many months of being sick and with complications from a tonsillectomy surgery, I was given devastating news. I remember the doctor sitting across from me while I sat on the exam table. He had a look of concern and pity in his eyes when he said, "Arliss, you have Ehlers-Danlos syndrome and there is no cure." I sat there in stunned silence. The truth is that there was always a part of me that knew that I had greater than normal health concerns. I had gotten sick more easily than those around me, I had experienced chronic pain since the age of 10, and I just seemed to be tired all the time. Because the doctors that I had seen as a child and adolescent had never found anything in any of my lab tests or medical exams, I had decided that it was just a form of weakness that I needed to overcome. **On that fall day in 2012, I learned that the way I had relentlessly pushed myself could cost me my life.**

At the time that I was diagnosed with Ehlers-Danlos Syndrome, I was very, very sick. I was using a wheelchair and walker because I had very little muscle mass and my hips would sublux or dislocate under the weight of my body when I walked. In follow-up visits, I learned that I had a football-sized mass in my intestines because my digestive system was not working properly. I had heart murmurs and other heart conditions. I was also having month-long menstrual periods and chronic ovarian cysts. I was on so many medications that I don't even remember them all. The doctor who originally diagnosed me told me, "I would be surprised if you lived more than two years. You should stop going to school and move to live with family so that they can care for you for the remainder of your life."

So that is what I did. I left the Neuroscience PhD program with a Master's degree, thanks to the unbelievable determination of my advisor. I sold 90%

of what I owned, found homes for my dogs, and moved to where my parents planned to retire, the Big Island of Hawaii. At that point, I honestly thought that my life was over. In truth, my life as I had known it up to that point, of pushing myself without any concern for my health or wellbeing, was over. I am overwhelmingly grateful that that is true today, but it would take me a long time to reach a grateful place.

It took putting my life on the line to learn to start to let go of the Pressure Myth. I would love to say that I never put myself under pressure, that I never overbook myself or never procrastinate but that is not true. I am learning this lesson in a deeper way all the time. I have learned about myself that when challenging things happen in my life or in the world around me, I can easily fall into a pattern of overdoing. This is a way for me to feel like I am making a difference and accomplishing something, even when things feel out of my control. The pandemic was a great example of this. I started doing all the things and guess what: I put myself under pressure and my health and wellbeing suffered. The brighter side of the pandemic for me was an even deeper learning experience around how to recognize when I am putting myself under pressure and how to release that stress. Here is what I learned.

Your Brain Under Stress

I am fascinated with the brain, and as a graduate neuroscience student, I read a lot about how the brain functions under stress (or doesn't). What I have learned has changed my life! According to research done at Harvard University, being under stress can negatively impact your brain function and memory (Harvard Health Publishing, 2021). Stress can create a disruption in the synapse regulation in our brains. Synapses are where two nerve cells come together and communicate through neurotransmitters. These synapses are connections in our brains that allow us to have thoughts and feelings. Our prefrontal cortex—the part of the brain which is responsible for decision-making, memory, and learning—is negatively affected by stress. Extreme and chronic stress can cause brain cells to die (McEwen, *Chronic Stress*, 2017). What?!? I know right! Talk about good motivation to stop buying into the Pressure Myth and reduce our stress.

Noticing When You Are Adding the Pressure

The first step in making a change is to notice when you are putting yourself under pressure. Take a moment and ask yourself if any of these indications of pressure are true for you:

- Your self-talk (your internal monologue) is very negative or critical
- When you do not meet your expectations (whether realistic or not), you are highly critical and angry toward yourself
- While sitting at your desk, you find it hard to keep an upright straight-backed posture
- You are noticing physical manifestations of your stress
- It is hard to maintain a regular sleep schedule
- You experience feelings of exhaustion
- You have times when you question whether people really like you
- You feel hair-trigger or on edge
- You have stopped taking good care of yourself and making self-care a priority

If you have noted that some, many, or all these things are true for you, do not be hard on yourself. The first step to making a change is noting that a change is needed. Try being gentle with yourself and showing under-standing and self-compassion to yourself. You are not alone. It is not too late. You can make a change. Let's dive into what it looks like in our brain when we reduce our stress.

Your Brain When You Reduce Stress

According to a study in the journal *Nature*, we learn better and have better memory when our brain is in a relaxed state (Raypole, *Nature*, 2021). In addition, being in a relaxed state has positive effects both mentally and physically. When relaxed, we have a lower respiration rate, have more endorphin release, have slower brain waves which allows for rejuvenation in our brain's chemistry, and our immune system functions better. Now that is some major motivation to let go of stress and pressure.

Solutions to Relieve Pressure and Stress

I learned the hard way through a major health crash about the Pressure Myth. But you don't have to take yourself to the brink like I did. You can start applying some simple solutions (or Soullutions!) in your life and business right now to take the pressure off and perform at your best. Here's some simple practices that work for me:

- **Practice mindfulness with your time**—mindfulness (noun): *The quality or state of being conscious or aware of something.* Before I say yes to something today, I stop and think. Is this realistic for me? Do I actually want/need/feel excited about doing this? I am more intentional about how I spend my precious time.
- **Schedule everything (including self-care and fun!)**—I schedule everything, EVERYTHING I want in my life on my phone, which is synced with my calendar on my computer. In the past, I used to only schedule work tasks, or important events. Now I schedule in my self-care time, fun time, breaks from work (I like to call this recess!). The positive impact this has on my daily life is pretty amazing!
- **Use scheduling links**—when booking calls and meetings for my business, I use my Calendly scheduling link. I have my calendar set up and synced with my scheduling software. This saves me time on back and

forth and also ensures that people are booking with me at times that are best for me.

- **Set two deadlines**—I front-load work by setting two deadlines and work periods for myself. For instance, let's say I'm writing a speech to give at a conference. I set one early deadline and work period for myself 10 days before the conference. Then, I set a second deadline and work period for three days before the conference. If I meet the first deadline, I reward myself. I schedule something fun for the second work period.
- **Reward yourself**—like I said above, I reward myself for getting things done early, instead of just filling my extra time with more work. I reward myself every time I complete a goal. Rewarding ourselves is scientifically linked to better performance.

HOW TO MOTIVATE WITHOUT PRESSURE

We have learned that pressure is actually an extremely poor motivator and negatively impacts us in many ways. So, how do we motivate ourselves without the use of pressure? We do this through the use of true confidence, resiliency, and knowing our capacity. Grow your confidence by celebrating your wins, noting your accomplishments, monitoring your progress along the way toward your goals, and act within your core values. Increase your resiliency by practicing self-compassion, building strong and positive relationships with others, and asking for help when needed. Know your capacity by being realistic about your time and energy, try not to do more than two-thirds of what you are capable of (that way you have reserves for when 100% is needed), try new things, and have a growth mindset.

Now do you believe you work better under pressure? I bet not and neither do I. I am always learning this in a deeper way and I invite you to start your journey of letting go of the Pressure Myth today.

Arliss Dudley-Cash MA, MBA

Winner of the Best Presentation Award by the International Women's Leadership and Empowerment Conference, Business and Self-Love Coach Arliss Dudley-Cash is an inspirational speaker and self-love movement leader. With a background in business, neuroscience and forensics, her career expands over several industries, including operations management, research scientist, and death investigation. Arliss unites this eclectic background with her personal journey to overcome the odds and survive a terminal diagnosis. Her award-winning presentations include topics on extreme self-love and body positivity. Arliss is a big believer in the magic of our individual stories and the power of storytelling to effect positive change in this world. In 2021, she co-founded The Body Positivity Podcast which she hosts with her colleague Diana Gremillion. Through her company Soullutions LLC, she is passionate about helping her clients to become powerful, joyful, authentic business owners experiencing freedom, having a lot more fun in their business, and experiencing the success of their dreams. In her free time, you can find her in the Pacific Ocean, painting, or playing with her three chihuahuas—Tonks, Moony, and Fluffy—on the beautiful Big Island of Hawaii with her partner, Matthew. Arliss's dream is for each of us to become the loves of our lives!

www.soullutions.com
Instagram: **@arliss_dudley_cash** & **@soul_utions** & **@bodypositivitypodcast**
Facebook: Soullutions Consulting & The Body Positivity Podcast
LinkedIn: Arliss Dudley-Cash & Soullutions & Body Positivity Podcast
arliss@soullutions.com
(209) 471-4947

WHEN LIFE PAUSED
BY CAROLYN J. DOUGLAS

"To believe your own thought, to believe that what is true for you
in your private heart is true for all men,—that is genius. Speak
your latent conviction, and it shall be the universal sense; for the
inmost in due time becomes the outmost,—and our first thought
is rendered back to us by the trumpets of the Last Judgment."
—Ralph Waldo Emerson

Seeing the brighter side of the pandemic takes a bit of forethought and introspection. After almost three years of living through this situation, I have formed a few thoughts around the experience of living with this threat to our way of life. My thoughts about it come from the things I see and believe through my own lens of awareness. I believe others can relate to my stories and may see something similar from their own stories about living during the pandemic time.

Picture this, the first quarter of 2020 became one of the most challenging times people in my various communities experienced. A global pandemic was declared. When we received the health and safety order to shelter in place, a range of emotions was felt on the visceral level from panic to relief. We were dealing with an unknown nemesis, a virus that was wreaking havoc on the lives of humans. Not too much was known about its origin or its transmission. It was causing chaos and not the harmony we loved to profess. Even my friends who work in healthcare services were freaking out. But they, in their commitment to life, were rising to the occasion to be helpful and resourceful. And I found myself looking for and purchasing face masks for the visiting nurses in our congregation to have so they could continue to provide at-home services to their clients.

At the spiritual center where I attend, the weekly gathering is lived for. A group of us was in the process of cleaning up and sanitizing the room, chairs, and the various pieces of equipment and implements used when the order came to shelter in place. Panic immediately set in. The question, "How do we do Sunday service now," was immediately on the lips of the crew.

We had just spent a few good hours diligently cleaning up the place to ensure our members entered a safe place. This order changed everything. Since we had experimented with livestreaming our program, that became an instantaneous, viable option. And we "pivoted on the dime"; an email message was sent out to our attendees on how to connect to the program. That was the beginning of a new way of doing our Sunday services. And the attendees showed up. It was just one innovation to establishing what was to become a new reality in how we came together in spiritual community. I hesitated at the time to call it a new normal. But to this date, the condition still exists. We've had false starts at reestablishing what used to be the normal way of coming together. Yet, I have been told that some of us love getting up, getting our cup of coffee or tea, cutting on the computer, and connecting into the Sunday Service and the online community gathering that follows. We are still able to be with one another even though we prefer to do it in person.

I view the "shelter in place" order as a big collective pause. Everything stopped for everyone. Our normal way of conducting our day, our very lives changed by a simple decision made by a group of government officials. It was done, of course, for our collective good. And, **I chose to see it in a more in-depth light. It was a life "pause" and there is a personal meaning for each person if one chooses to reach for it.**

The origin of the word *pause* means to stop. That is what happened. Life as we knew it was stopped. We stopped our usual, normal daily life activities and held our breath as feelings of uncertainty tightened their grip around us. As the days grew into weeks, months, and now years, the uncertainty of what's next still looms before us. It is like Mother Nature Herself sent us to our rooms to sit and contemplate our existence. From the perspective of the environment, there came an obvious sign of cleaner and better air quality. It has been attributed to the significant reduced number of automobiles on the roadways, putting hydrocarbon emissions into the air. That is a wonderful awakening and benefit to our collective life. Fresh, cleaner air to breathe, what a benefit!

Along with this cessation, there were the personal losses of workplace, friends and loved ones, routines, and subroutines. But I began to form newer awarenesses. For example, the people in my neighborhood changed over time due to the children growing up, moving off to college, followed by the parents' downsizing the home and moving away. There were now newer people in my neighborhood that I saw but did not know by name. There had not been a relationship established between us. There was no sense of community with them.

I personally had discontent with my own home. To bring it up to modern standards would cost just as much or more than purchasing a new one. My two sons are grown and off living their own lives. I mentioned my discontent to one of them and he referred me to a professional he was working with to purchase a new home for his family. Working with an agent, I placed my home on the market for sale. I got a reasonable contract on the first day of the open house and moved into my new home within a month's time. This was amazing. It seemed like the interruption in my normal life was bringing about newer, good things, ushering me into a newer way of being. I attribute this to the current state in which we are living. This is good. As I think it through clearly, **I released and let go of what was no longer serving me and became open to receive something that would serve me better.**

In this moment, I acknowledged to myself that I was shapeshifting. Shapeshifting is a term used by some storytellers to describe the ability to transform oneself through an inherent ability. If you connect to folklore, fairy tales, fantasy tales and the like, you will see the hero or heroine of the story go through challenges which eventually transform them from one way of being to another. **It is a growth opportunity that is quite beneficial to the soul of that person. After settling into my new home, I felt re-created and ready to live a new life.**

Now, if this experience meant that to me, I began to wonder how this pandemic situation was impacting others. I began to ask my friends and associates the question, "What good has come as a result of your changing so drastically?" It never failed that I received some consistent answers.

"I am more peaceful." "I don't have to rush around anymore." "Thank Goodness for the rest." "I've started my own business." "I am my own boss. I have my own schedule." "I have the time to do the things I really love and I don't feel guilty about it." "I never knew working at home would be a reality and work for me."

I was most impressed by one of my associates, Marian (fictitious name), who shared that she took the time to go within through a meditative process to discern what changes she should make for advancement in her career. Since that time, she has followed her intuition and is on track for her next level of growth in her profession. Removed from the hustle and bustle of working in an office environment, she has time to think, reflect on her choices and proceed with deliberate intent to succeed every time. And she is content with her own assessment as she sees herself advancing by both her standard and her company's standard.

Now her story demonstrates self-satisfaction. So, I asked what her process was for doing this. She shared her tips to succeed with deliberate intention in today's world:

1. Every day without fail, give thanks for everything, that which you know and expect and that which is an unknown and unexpected occurrence
2. Call or name everything good no matter what. Some unknown good has to be knocking at your door
3. Meditate at least 15 minutes each day to center yourself and remind yourself of your purpose, your cause, and your intent
4. Lastly, journal your thoughts from your meditation and keep track of the newer good things that are happening that demonstrate advancement within you and your career

I find this is a simple process that can easily be followed to bring about change in your life.

The more I consider, perhaps, what is the purpose of the pandemic, I keep getting the thought that it is about change and that change leads to transformation. In this regard, let me share another story from another one of my associates, Agnes (a fictitious name).

Agnes has lived a very prosperous life. It has been filled with abundance and opulence. Now that the pandemic has forced change upon many, she came to the place in her thinking where she felt she did not need or want all that excess. It had well served the purpose in attracting people and things to her. She no longer felt she needed it. This led to downsizing her quantity of stuff and finding a place that met her specific living needs. And, she found a lovely home for rent that is an in-law suite on a larger property which included a beautiful garden area where she could sit and enjoy nature or plant flowers and watch them grow.

Agnes was only content for a very short time before she started crying and whining about her discontent. It seemed that everything was going wrong, and when I asked what specifically was wrong, we developed a strategy for making the situation better. It appeared we had a plan of action for a better situation when she'd start crying and whining again about things not being right or working out. I reminded her of the plan of action and that good things were already in place for the good she wanted to experience to happen. It really meant just waiting for the appointed time to come about. Well, that was not sufficient. And her continual crying and discontent identified new, unrelated issues to the first problem. It seemed the more things she began to see as problems, the more miserable her life was becoming. Settled in a garden of beauty, Agnes was miserable over minor, minute things. This went on for a while until I asked what she was grateful for. To which she replied, "It was hard to find anything to be grateful for." I was astonished to hear her say those words. Then I asked, "With so many things going so wrong, what is it that you really want? Just tell me and we will try to figure out a solution." To this, Agnes reluctantly replied she was fearful that she would lose her connections and that no one would be there for her. Hearing this authentic confession, I replied to Agnes that from now on, every day she should call me and tell me at least one thing that she is grateful for. I would be there to listen. She agreed. So far, we are both keeping our part of the bargain.

As I think further on her story, I realize it was somewhat of a shock to her system of thought to realize that now the material trappings were gone, most of the people were gone too. For too long, much of her identity had been held in what she had that people wanted to be associated with rather than in who she is as an authentic person, a valuable resource in the lives of others. What an awakening to the self! What an opportunity to venture into the depths of the soul to see what else could be revealed about who she has come here to be.

In each one of the stories shared, there has been some beneficial shape-shifting. And, if you prefer, there has been some form of beneficial transformation. To simply sum up the main message of the story: **Before the pandemic, I used to be one way, now I am another and it serves me well.** Perhaps the interruption in the old life needed to happen for something new and better to come through. Ouch! How often does this sort of thing have to happen for one to come to a realization to make a change for the better? In each case, real good is showing up for all concerned. The seriousness that we now apply to our lives, while being mindful of the impact and influence of the pandemic, has caused a great many to reassess and realize what is truly important to them. It has caused many to let go of the hum of our pre-pandemic life to embrace the beauty of now, to see what is right before us, to see what we want, and how we want to live.

I am inspired by these moments of clarity that have eked out through the morass of competing thoughts. It is through these moments of clarity that one rises in their own greatness of being. Unfortunately, it is easier to hear complaints about a situation than to give credit for something good coming from it. I have hope that more good will continue to show itself in our personal lives. I recognize on a global scale that we are interconnected, for the pandemic is far-reaching and is not a respecter of persons. It infects the human body regardless of location or any of the other stuff we use to separate ourselves. Hence, it is my intent and purpose to continue looking for the ways the pandemic has brought out the brighter side in another's life.

In my closing thought, I choose to be reminded of the words of Ralph Waldo Emerson, "To believe your own thought, to believe that what is true for you in your private heart is true for all men—that is genius." **I choose to believe in the privacy of my heart, the good I want for myself is the good that I want for others. It matters not if it is a certain style of living, a certain way of being in the world, or coming to a personal realization of your own value. Know yourself!**

Pandemic or not, my intention is to see the brighter side of life for everyone. Be well. Embrace who you truly are and let your brighter light shine.

Carolyn J. Douglas

Carolyn J. Douglas is a graduate of the University of San Francisco with a Master's in Environmental Management and a graduate of Holmes Institute of Graduate Studies with a Master's of Divinity. She worked for several years as a civilian employee of the Unites States federal government through the Veterans Administration, the U.S. Department of the Navy, and the U.S. Environmental Protection Agency. Her work experience and skills include workshop presenter/facilitator, project management, contracting and project officer. She is currently a certified professional with the HeartMath Institute with a specialty in building personal resilience and resilience advantage. She teaches coherence breathing and meditation techniques to support heart-based living.

Carolyn Douglas is an ordained minister with Centers for Spiritual Living since 2004, serving as senior minister and spiritual director for Firelight Church of Religious Science, Illuminata Spiritual Center and now Center for Spiritual Living Peninsula. Beyond the local center, she has served as a Regional Support Coordinator to CSL ministers and centers in the Northern California area. She is an active Board Member of the International New Thought Alliance and a charter member of the People of African Descent New Thought where she serves on the planning and program teams. Carolyn is a Distinguished Toastmaster, joining in 2012. She has served in several club officer and district leadership roles. She is currently serving as a District 57 Director in the Northern California area. In her personal life she is a thought leader and assists nonprofit organizations in building their leadership capabilities and capacity.

Further, Carolyn Douglas is a co-author with three stories in *Every Woman Has a Short Story, Men Too!* with lead author Lille McGhee-Queen. She contributes inspirational thought weekly to her center's newsletter.

Facebook page: **www.facebook.com/carolyn.douglas.7330**
Facebook page: HeartFirst Coherence Meditation
Website: **www.cslpeninsula.org**

CREATING LIGHT FROM DARKNESS
BY MARCELA CORDOVA

Demonic figures were always present in my dreams or so I thought. Sometimes I would be awake and these things would be staring at me with piercing dark yellow-red eyes, paralyzing me to the point of excruciating pain in the body, especially in my throat. Throughout my childhood, I got to see many of these entities with different personalities and voices. All of their intentions were the same, which was implementing fear and trying to get into my space.

Growing up and talking about these things would make me sound crazy, so I kind of convinced myself that they were just nightmares. The professionals I was working with related them to the trauma that happened to me in my younger years. Yes, I was abused by many people; caretakers, family members, and acquaintances of adults I knew, both men and women, the majority of them being men. I couldn't form speech at an early age, which might have made me an easy target. In fact, some of my first clear sentences were when I was six years old. When each trauma event took place, I would cry hysterically and people would say I'm an annoying kid and or that I needed to be taught some discipline. One could say that with a lot of trauma, people create their own reality.

It didn't help that I had certain abilities that made me vulnerable to the other side as well. Growing up I would see the entities morph themselves into the people I knew in my daily life. I would see images of maggots, centipedes, spiders, snakes, fangs, scales, and horns on my abusers. Sometimes horrific creatures near them or embodied in them. At times, I blacked out because of the extreme terror running through my body as the abuse was happening. I blacked out somewhere in the course of each abuse episode.

I had disturbing dreams; some of them would actually predict future scenarios (precognitions). It would either protect me for the next day or the next few days, weeks, or months. I tried to ignore the dreams or tried to find scientific reasons behind all these images but couldn't find explanations for them.

The help with my clairvoyance, telepathic, and precognitive side came in at age 14. My mother heard about this Shaman woman on the radio who hosted seminars in the Bay Area; we will call her Tonya. My mother wanted to go to one of Tonyas' seminars and she invited me to come along. She's always been intrigued about the spiritual side of things. I was excited that I was going to go attend something like this. There were 35 people at the seminar. In the beginning, we did some cleansing rituals, meditation and chanting.

About two hours into the seminar, we were all sitting on the floor holding hands in a cross-legged position. I started to feel discomfort in the base of my spine. I tried to adjust my sitting position but the pain kept feeling worse. The pain was rising up to my upper body and I was starting to sweat. I started to yell and scream because it was too much torment to contain. Tonya put her hands on my forehead and told me to "let him in." Within moments, I felt like my spine was ripping in half and something was coming out of it. I screamed from the top of my lungs and something else took over the center of my head. The entity was possessing my body. The sounds it made through my body were unnatural and beast-like. The lights started to flicker and my chest felt like a microphone echoing the sound of this creature speaking through me. As this was happening, I could see from the back of my eyes yet this entity was maneuvering my body and speaking through me. Tonya declared that this was a demon and that it was in my space causing a lot of suffering.

From age 14 to 21, I had what I thought was a mother-and-daughter relationship with Tonya. It felt good to have someone acknowledge that the things I see were real and that she could see them too. There were points in this relationship that were toxic. She often said that she was going to die at any point and that there was no one as powerful as her in the world. I asked her, "What will happen to me if you die? How will I maintain my space clear of these entities?" to which she responded, "You could possibly find someone out there but it won't be me, they are hard to find." I then would ask her if I could learn what she knows so that I wouldn't have to suffer in case she dies. I wanted to be able to take care of myself. Her response was always "I am the medium, you are a portal. I am born with the spiritual abilities, you are not. You can never learn what I know." After several conflicts, she cut ties with me. She told me that I still had the demon inside me and that she would keep a candle lit for me. I believe I started asking too many questions and that's what led her to push me away. I was terrified thinking I needed her for my own survival. I feared the world of these frightening entities as if they had power over me. I became very anxious.

I eventually found a spiritual teacher that created a space of sanctuary and gave my spirit and body permission to find its harmony on its own time. I will call her Judy. She introduced me to clairvoyance, healing, and owning my own energetic space. Before I became her student, I would go to her for intuitive readings or a hands-on healing session. It felt like I was seen and that everything validated my own personal spiritual journey. I was introduced to running my own energy and setting space. Grounding was very essential for me. Seeing colors, figures, and energies came naturally to me but in a controlled and safe space was something so new to me. I was gaining confidence in managing my spiritual tools.

During one of my phone classes with Judy, I experienced confronting one of my biggest fears. I saw an entity appear in my space and I started freaking out. I let Judy know about this entity. I thought I was going to die. In sheer terror, I asked if I could drive to her place since I knew where she lived. She paused and then agreed to have me come over. I rushed to her house as fast as I could. I was not able to control my emotions. I was preparing myself for excruciating pain again, thinking that the process of taking whatever is in my space out would be like Tonyas' exorcisms.

Judy was still teaching class but she asked the co-teacher to take over while Judy offered support to me. In a strong voice, Judy told me to sit down, then sit up straight. I was hunched over in my seat protecting myself. I hesitated to sit upright. I told her that I couldn't do it because the visual of the being was incapacitating. Judy told me to sit up straight and tell it who's boss. She said, "You have the body. You are senior in yourself and everything that is not you." Judy reassured me that I was in control of my own space and that I have every right to own the center of my head. No one else has that right. She was giving me some tough love. She was reassuring me that I do have the capability to run my tools and own my own space. I had the power to heal myself.

I was calming down as I set my crown to gold, she mentioned that this being was a tiny little bean making itself appear big and ferocious. Basically, she was telling me how much more powerful I am compared to these beings who tend to cause chaos. When I graduated from Judys' course, she referred me to another school. As much as she enjoyed having me, she believed I should make many connections and not rely on just one. She also affirmed that I have my own unique truth and that when the time comes, I will live it. She also introduced me to the idea that someone may outgrow their mentors and/or as one becomes closer to another (friendship), it's best to divest oneself. To this day, Judy and I are great friends!

I signed up for new courses at this school that I will call Aragon. Classes took place over the phone. I still had a fear of seeing intense energies in my space, but I felt better knowing that I had a support system around me. The teachers were fabulous and so funny! I was then starting to feel a bit off in my life. I was feeling the "growth period" where I was working a lot of energies and coming into new steps in life in general. I felt the intensity of life! I decided to talk to one of the head people from Aragon, seeing if they could give me their input on what I should do. I needed communication about my "growth period." I talked to the wrong person that day because I was crying and sounding very depressed and they didn't want to associate themselves with someone with mental illness. I reassured them that I was OK with taking classes and continuing on. I knew in that moment that I needed a "hello" to my spirit. They were hesitant to allow me to continue my journey at Aragon. They had the power to do so. I was extremely confused because Judy explained that back in her day, people went through a lot of emotions when working their energetic tools and experiencing "growing pains." This is the place that Judy graduated from a long time ago! I was taking a course on chakras. Each month, there was a chakra in focus. How surprising that I had to stop during the third chakra month! That's when I was feeling my most intense moments! This showed me that I had a lot to work when it came to my third chakra which is my will, my confidence, and how I live my life in this world.

After this school experience, I shied away from spirituality. I still kept meditating but not as much. I felt humiliated and lost some hope in my situation.

I was introduced to Cody Edner. He offered classes and services in intuitive reading and healing, spiritual deprogramming, and transmedium healing. I scheduled a session with Cody.

In 2020, the pandemic hit. Everyone was to quarantine in their homes for the time being. Surfing the web, I found a great astrologer, The Modern Daoist by the name Adrian Lim. I scheduled a Zoom appointment with him. Beforehand, I gave him my birthdate info and he read my Bazi and Zi Wei Dou Shu charts which read my past and present so accurately! A huge reason why I went to him was because he seemed grounded by his reviews. His website showed he knew his craft. I wanted some practical, logical, spiritual information in front of me. My charts had their own unique suggestions in how I could align myself with my gifts. Our conversation was heartwarming and amusing. Adrian suggested that mediation and developing my spiritual abilities would benefit me for my higher purpose, especially when it came to my health. He was amazed at what my intuition could do and where it could potentially lead me. To this day, we still communicate with one another!

In 2021 during the pandemic, I signed up for Energy Matters Academy founded by David Gandelman and Cody Edner. David is the author of *The Seven Energies of the Soul* and the founder of the Meditation School App. I knew I was in good hands! This course helps individuals awaken to their spiritual abilities in a safe and healthy manner. I wanted to go through all four parts of the program. I committed myself for a whole year of practicing how to manage my energetic tools, self-heal, and live with my own certainty. The beginning of my course included building a solid foundation in spiritual connection with the body and mind, distinguishing what is my energy vs. foreign energy, releasing and receiving energy, and becoming certain within my space. A big part of this training was to teach students how to "see" and "read" energy in meditation. This triggered my terrifying history of seeing entities. I panicked every time I encountered these intense energies. I had to have teachers assist me in reclaiming my space. Grounding became my best friend! I did truly love the program and how much I loved to participate! Seeing came naturally for me. It was a treat to see things through the vibration of amusement. Building friendships in class really encouraged me to keep moving forward. When other students expressed where they were at emotionally, it gave me the sense of connection and oneness. One of my greatest friends I met through the academy was Melissa Sabino; we shared many laughs and personal challenges together. She is an amazing kundalini yoga teacher and energy worker. I ended up graduating on the first of May 2022. I successfully graduated the Intuitive Training Program of Energy Matters Academy. I am authorized to give intuitive spiritual counseling, readings and healings. I didn't take this program to become a licensed clairvoyant. I took this program to help heal myself and manage my abilities. I discovered that I have gone through a lot of turmoil to reclaim my personal power and spiritual abilities. Knowing that I have this gift, I may have children or grandchildren that may inherit this as well. I want to be there for them whereas no one was there for me when I was young. I realize as I do this, I also heal past generations and break cycles especially for the women that came before me.

I continue on this journey. I recently completed the Align and Heal Program with Brandon Wilcox. I now give intuitive readings where I give your spirit a "hello" and help you bring your awareness to your space in your body and spirit. I communicate where your energy is in alignment with your path. I can help you look into your next step with clarity and, most of all, connection to your own personal truth. This truth aligns you to your own unique journey. Thank you so much for reading my story! And the rest is continuing to be written . . .

Marcela Cordova

Marcela Cordova is based in the Bay Area. She has won many art and literary awards. She is a professional face and body painter since the age of 10. She is CEO of Fascinating Face and Body Painting. Her slogan is "I can paint Anything you ask!"

Her Instagram is @FascinatingFaceandBodyPainting and her Facebook page is "Fascinating Face and Body Painting." She has degrees in communications and dance. She is a certified yoga teacher. She is continuing her studies at San Francisco State University and Majoring in Kinesiology. She gives professional Intuitive readings through her business "Readings by Ella" (Instagram: @Readingsby_Ella).

Resources:
Energy Matters Academy: **https://energymattersacademy.com/**
Cody Edner: **https://www.intuitivevision.net/**
David Gandelman: **https://www.meditationschool.us/**
Lada Ballowe: **https://www.ladaballowe.com**
Brandon Wilcox: **https://brandonjwilcox.com/**
Jason Seiler: **https://calendly.com/jason-seiler/clairvoyant-reading**

Kale Sanders: **stefen.intuitivecounseling@gmail.com**
Marjorie Bratt: **https://intuicionactiva.com/intuicion-activa/**
Adrian Lim: **https://www.themoderndaoist.com/**
Melissa Sabino: Instagram **@melissasabino_embody**

MIND OVER MOUNTAIN
BY SHANNON SUNDBERG

As I reflect on the beginning of the isolation and the unknowns that seemed to be endless, I remember thinking there was no way I'd survive being isolated and shut down for two weeks. As it extended into longer time periods, I questioned what I could handle and whether I would make it through.

The first few days, I sat in disbelief and played every "what if" scenario in my head about my business, my home, my family and my life. I kept trying to predict what I would do when things cleared up and how big of a mess I would have. The first few days in isolation, I sat frozen in fear and panic. Nothing was getting done and I wasn't taking action in any aspect beyond caring for the family.

The question of what to do kept replaying in my head. I didn't know and that scared me. I didn't have a path planned out; I was feeling lost and unprepared. I knew that something had to happen but everything I knew to do wasn't an option. My job was supporting people in their wellness journey, done in person with footbaths, frequency & aromatherapy sessions, biocommunication scans, feeling the energy in the room and creating a plan to carry them forward in their journey. I had the belief I couldn't do that without being in the same space with them. How else could I support them? I had to figure out something to keep them, myself and my family supported. I felt stuck.

Even in isolation, quiet time wasn't abundant with having four people in our household, so I started spending time in the garden to have quiet and alone time. There were no demands in the garden; I could sit, listen and let myself reset. My intuitive side started calming and soothing the fear and anxiety that seemed to be taking over my days. Hands in the dirt, planting and watching growth from a seed . . . that was buried and I waited to see if it would emerge from the darkness. As the sprouts started emerging through the dirt, so did the realization that I had an opportunity to become anything I dreamed of right now. **I could be a seed, emerge from the darkness and grow into something beautiful that gives nourishment and hope to others; I just had to start. I had to take action, so I committed to three actions each day focused on connecting my mind, body, and spirit.**

I buried myself in dreams, hope, wishes and love, connecting with my heart to discover what's been glossed over during my busy days of being a mother, wife, daughter, sister and entrepreneur. Always rushing between responsibilities, now I had few demands and plenty of time to feel into my future. My first obstacle was to overcome the paralyzing fear that had taken over my thoughts from the moment I opened my eyes each morning and kept me awake each night. My fear was a steep mountain with a precarious narrow path winding back and forth with sharp stones and landslides hindering the climb to the summit. The mountain seemed formidable but I knew I had to see the other side; the glimmer of hope that there's a greater purpose for me on the other side drove me into action.

The first action steps were to support myself and my son as we navigated distance learning. Creating the setting and atmosphere to be successful went beyond a clean learning space with appropriate tools. The space needed to promote focus, safety, and harmony. I harnessed my aromatherapy experience and created *Harmony at Home & Gentle Day AromaCare* packages that included Atmosphere sprays, Rollerball blends, and soothing Bath soaks. Using the spray as soon as I got up each morning supported my outlook for each day, while the rollerball helped me last through the afternoons. Starting with my own self care created a daily habit that I could share with my family. Spraying in the room to start school and rolling on after lunch and body breaks put all of us on the road to success. **This action of self care for creating the best atmosphere to thrive was the first step in overcoming the continued challenges of having life shut down.** Our school time transformed from dread and arguing into daily accomplishments and high fives. My action steps trampled my fears of failing my son and brought inspiration and harmony into our home. Each time I used my signature Happy spray, the smiles became contagious and joy smoothed over the sharp area on the pathway to ease my journey up the mountain.

Taking some schooling outside, this freedom brought us into the garden more and more, providing opportunities to grow food to nourish our bodies along with herbs and flowers for therapeutic benefits. Each of us gained different comforts from being in the garden so my next action steps for expanding the garden created a common goal in building not only the physical raised beds, but a greater purpose in our choices and intentions. Soon we were harvesting food, herbs, and flowers to make infusions, tonics, balms, soaks, and scrubs. **The garden developed into a peaceful space that welcomed each of us to reset our mind, body, and spirit with the gifts it provided with food, herbs, and creativity.** The garden became our source of stamina for our journey up the steep mountain.

As life settled into a new routine, I turned my next action steps towards my business and creating ways to serve within the limitations. Seeking connection with other like-minded women, virtual gatherings became a highlight as I gained inspiration, ideas and comfort. Pushing through my tech challenges and embracing the virtual stage brought a new world of possibilities of being together across the nation. **Going virtual was awkward, uncomfortable and yet opened a vision of a limitless horizon. A path I had never considered because it never seemed necessary was now very needed and expanded my reach from local driving distance to the potential of serving women worldwide.** Opening my mind to this new opportunity with support from family and friends helped widen my path up the mountain and I stepped into the beauty of many new connections and relationships that started out as just a face on a screen. My seed was sprouting and these wins were providing what my mind, body and spirit needed to keep pushing through the steep darkness to the flickering light of hope, growing and becoming stronger with each step.

With six months of isolation behind me, opening to discovering new opportunities was gaining momentum and taking daily action steps was propelling me into new realms of experience and knowledge. I completed two Life Coach certifications that focused on creating life balance with the intention of becoming a better version of ourselves each day, each month, each year. This huge accomplishment carried me to another goal of completing my Master Reiki training. This brought a deepened awareness and confidence, while pushing the fear and panic out of my "what-ifs." Suddenly, I was heading into the holidays with a new set of "what-ifs" that were driven by hope, inspiration and dreams. My AromaCare packages became Aromatic gift boxes bringing joy, harmony, and gentle days to many. I began to embrace the serenity that came with practicing Reiki and started offering distance healing on the virtual stage that had quickly grown into a welcoming and comfortable space for me. Growing confident in my intuitive talents was the fuel I needed to continue up the mountain, giving me the energy and agility to climb over the obstacles on the path.

The last leg of my journey seemed insurmountable. While I was able to find gratitude in all the situations along the way, the path seemed narrow with boulders of doubt, concern, and even self-sabotage. The daily actions helped me strengthen new and existing friendships, create a harmonious family nourished with food we grew together, become open to discovering and growing my services and creating new streams of revenue, and yet I still had worry for what was to come. I was growing comfortable in my new lifestyle, yet my progress slowed as I glimpsed the diffused rays of sunlight. I had emerged from the soil and was opening to the world and seeking the confirmation of sunlight to continue growing. What was holding me back from the crest of this mountain?

First, let me share this story:

***

Through the isolation, I began training to run a half marathon . . . for a third time. The first time I injured my ankle shortly before the race and the second time, I was blessed with being pregnant with my son and advised not to do the race while six months pregnant. As I was building momentum with my daily actions and having confidence in my accomplishments of new dreams and goals, I had to revisit this unfinished goal from ten years ago. I joined a virtual training program and showed up for race day feeling prepared and excited. I started out strong and confident; the surroundings were beautiful. Around mile 4, the bladder in my water pack started leaking but I worked through it and continued. At mile 6, my phone battery warns it's at 20%. I was running GPS and music and it quickly drained my battery. Continuing only with GPS, I made it to the turn-around point and knew I could find my way back if the phone shut off—which happened around mile 10. As I approach the last leg of this journey, I start having doubts I can make it back. My body and mind are at odds over finishing. There's that voice saying you've tried before and couldn't do it. The voice continues to say I didn't train hard enough or long enough, just stop running, you're out of water. I start walking and crying. I keep moving forward even as the voice gets louder saying it's okay to give up. I see the turn for the last leg; another racer is heading out. It's a face from a screen that I've seen dozens of times through our virtual program. Greetings and encouraging words are shared in quick passing. I don't remember the exact words but I remember that 10-second interaction gave me the push to continue. My mind and body became aligned in the determination to finish strong. I heard a voice again, different this time; it was saying to be strong and courageous. I finished the half marathon and accomplished my goal.

***

To continue up my mountain, I had to get in the right mindset. Words are powerful and that voice that speaks to us that no one else hears can hurt our progress or propel us. I needed to have the faith and belief in myself that I had trained and prepared enough to finish the half marathon. **I now needed to trust in myself and be my own cheerleader in making it to the crest of my mountain. The doubts and self-sabotage were replaced with strong and courageous affirmations, meditation and prayer and self-compassion.** My daily actions now include saying positive and inspiring words to myself, transposing doubtful words with encouraging words. My progress to the crest of the mountain continued with intention and purpose. I accomplished my goal of connecting my mind, body, and spirit along my path. **I pushed past just surviving to be thriving. I didn't settle into despair and fear of the unknown.** I moved forward into the unknown with hope, love, and an open heart and mind, creating the welcoming atmosphere for success, positivity and support. Did I make it to the top? Yes! Yes, I did.

Mind over Mountain ~ just in time to enjoy my magical blue hour. I want you to know you too can make it to the top and move from surviving to thriving!

Shannon Sundberg

I am a passionate Mompreneur and love serving as a Hope Dealer & Mindset Mentor, bringing Mind, Body, and Spirit wellness together on a united path. I conquered my own limiting beliefs that blocked me and focused diligently on the areas that accelerated my progress towards my best life and my greater purpose. I love connecting with women and helping evaluate the 7 key areas in life and support them as they conquer the overwhelm and create their path to a Balanced life and work towards their dreams and goals. I provide guidance, support and alternative tools for my clients to go get what they truly want in life and know they deserve it. I started out as an Aromatherapist over 20 years ago, and over the last six years have added being a Reiki Master, Certified Oola Life Coach, and Certified Green Gap Coach.

Intuitive from a young age, I have been able to listen with my heart and be an energetic support for many. I'm passionate in my pursuit to serve others and my happiness is fueled with seeing others living in joy.

What sparks my joy is my husband and son. We enjoy camping, reading, laughing, hiking, fishing and especially gardening together.

Shannon Sundberg
Soily Aromatics, Energetics, and Mentoring

email: **soilyaromatherapy@gmail.com**
Website: **https://shannonsundbergcoach.com**
https://linktr.ee/shannonsundbergcoach
FB Page: **https://www.facebook.com/Soilyaromatherapy**
FB Group: Wellness From Within with Shannon Sundberg
https://www.facebook.com/groups/192939238674510/
Instagram: **https://www.instagram.com/soilyaromatherapy/**
LinkedIn: **https://www.linkedin.com/in/shannon-sundberg-soily-aromatics -and-energetics-82773637/**
Shop Soily Aromatics: **https://bit.ly/shopSoily**

FINDING HOPE IN CHAOS
BY DR. CONRAD MILLER

As a Jamaican engineer and entrepreneur, I have coined and duly accepted the name "The Business Engineer." This persona is one that has grown and evolved (ironically I might say!) since the start of the pandemic that began in the year 2019. As a father of two (2) special needs children, an entrepreneur, and an engineering manager in an intense, 7-days-a-week work environment, the pandemic could not have come at a worse time. It was Steve Jobs who reminded us that "in life, we can only connect the dots by looking backward." So I am about to share with you the small victories I enjoyed during this pandemic; but to do that, you must first understand the challenges I had to overcome.

THE STRUGGLES

After completing a Master's degree in Engineering Management, I decided, in 2017, to start a doctoral program that was originally due to be completed in the year 2020. Little did I know that the pandemic would hit in 2019, totally changing life as we knew it. Online or not, maneuvering a high-intensity academic program when the country was in total lockdown was no easy feat. I imagine maneuvering the new way of life was not easy for anyone, and I know many people worldwide faced this difficulty. I was lucky not to have been directly hit with the disease, but I unfortunately found myself in numerous situations where I needed to isolate my family and be engaged in testing to confirm my health.

Who can focus on reading numerous scholarly articles daily while wondering if anyone in your immediate family has caught a life-threatening disease? As if that was not enough, it became apparent just about this time as well, that the second of my two children (my daughter) was also on the severe end of the autism spectrum. I am sure dealing with neuro-divergent children is an ordeal in any country in the world; but in Jamaica, even testing a child for autism or any developmental challenges can be both expensive, exhausting and time-consuming for parents. As the patriarch of the family, many options floated around—"Should I migrate?", "Should I try enrolling them in a special, customized program or try intermingling them with 'typical' children?" All these added weights not just on my shoulders but on my brain. I was in no state to be enrolled in anything much less a higher education program. Hence, while doing this doctorate, I quickly lost my drive and forgot my reason for starting school despite being so excited when I had just started back in 2017.

It was not easy. In addition to being a full-time student, I was also working as an engineering manager at a demanding power plant where I worked most weekends. Not to forget, I also had to take care of my family. Having two children on the severe end of the autism spectrum is very demanding, stressful, and expensive. So, when the pandemic hit, it was, in fact, a perfect storm. My world came crashing down. You can also imagine that this must have taken a toll on my relationships and even my health declined. I had to make a decision: Should I continue with school? Or should I quit and refocus my attention on work and my family? In the end, I kept going despite all the challenges—much to the detriment of my physical and mental conditions.

Against that background, I suppose it would not surprise anyone that, while doing my doctorate (despite having a perfect GPA), **I was kicked out of school three times**. Yes, I was actually administratively removed from the university once for financial reasons and twice for "inadequate progress in dissertation milestones." I was unable to fund myself and had to take several bank loans, take a second mortgage on my house and finally take a loan from my dear Aunt Maxine. Asking someone for money was very difficult for me and an internal struggle I had to overcome; I typically (till then) was the stable one in the family that anyone could lean on for help. Yet, there I was . . . making a promise to return a payment knowing I had doubts I actually would.

It is quite natural and sensible to assume that someone living/working at their full capacity would stop there, but no. In 2021, I became obsessed with the notion of creating a mobile phone app that could improve audiences' engagement, especially in live settings. I woke up one day thinking of nothing but how to improve feedback from online viewers for normal social media content. **What was happening to me???** I am/was not a programmer, and so there started another journey that would take even more of my resources (financial, energy and time) that were already rationed. I decided to call the project I.A.N (Interactive Audience Network). The excitement I felt creating I.A.N arose from my drive to improve the lives of others through creativity.

How I Overcame These Struggles

So, how did I overcome all these struggles? It was not easy, but I had to find, again, my "why." My "why" is, was, and always will be my family. I wanted to set an example for my children—that no matter what life throws at you, you can always get back up and try again. I wanted to look into the eyes of my 94-year old grandmother and tell her what I had achieved. And so, **I kept going**. I kept on fighting to stay on track and eventually finished my doctorate in July 2022, despite all the odds being against me.

Therefore, whatever struggles you are facing, remember your "why." Why are you doing what you're doing? What is your purpose? This evasive "purpose" can sometimes be misleading, but once you have your "current why," nothing will be able to stop you. You will find the strength to overcome any obstacle. Just like I did. I followed a number of productive practices and habits to keep myself on track. These may help you as well:

Productive Practices & Habits

- **Daily** affirmations
- **Expression** through writing
- Listening to **uplifting videos** on social media
- Daily **meditation** and keeping the focus on my "why"
- Setting realistic **goals**
- Making **detailed plans** and sticking to them despite the mood/ feeling on the day
- Getting **rid of distractions**
- Recognizing my **support system**
- Remembering that "calm seas never made a **skilled sailor**"
- **Finding purpose** in every challenge, either to overcome or to learn; hence converting challenges from being a curse into a lesson

I believe that everyone needs some way to express themselves. It could be music, art, speaking, something. Mine was writing. And I chronicled all my worst moments. I got up at 5 am almost every day and wrote positive things (when I wasn't even feeling positive). Many times, I even cursed God in my writing but I know He understood my heart. But bottom line, when I wrote, it became my therapy, and my re-alignment to what "amazes me, amuses me, and what moves me." —Mark Brown

Looking back at how I overcame these struggles, three key things stand out:

One, build up on your support team.

I must mention the support I received from my family, especially my loving partner at home, Latoya Lobban. I know it wasn't easy for her to see me go through all that pain and stress. But she never gave up on me—not once did she complain. And this showed me that whatever we face, having the right person to face it with **does make a difference.** Choose to have people in your life, people who are willing to support you in your endeavors and are aligned with your dreams and goals.

Two, make time to grow, learn and discover what is most important to you.

If you have never watched the video clip about "big rocks," you should. Juggling between the many hats I donned, I became very occupied—with both big and small rocks. But no matter how "busy" I was with my "big rocks," I always made time to keep upgrading myself. I wasn't at all consistent about what I learned, but I kept learning. Every two weeks, I would **hyper-focus** on learning something for free on YouTube. And that kept my juices going. Or I would sign up (sometimes at my own cost) for a course or a program that I thought would be a useful skill to have. I haven't used them all yet . . . but I do believe that it helped take my mind off a stressful life and has helped me to become a more rounded individual. It certainly helped to form a very important thing needed for success and creativity, and that is PERSPECTIVE.

Three, have faith.

Also, the other quality one must have during hard times is an unshakable faith. Faith in yourself, your abilities, and most importantly, God. Because when everything else fails, your faith will be the only thing that will keep you going. And so, my dear reader, whatever challenges you are facing right now, **NEVER** give up. Remember your purpose, remember your "why" and have faith. Because I promise you, things will get better.

What I Achieved During the Pandemic

So finally, what did I REALLY achieve? Despite all the odds, I continued my journey and kept bettering myself. Amidst the chaos, I found peace. Through my conscious intention, pure dedication, unwavering faith, and never-give-up attitude, I achieved my goals and many great events manifested in my life. My hard work has paid off and I was even promoted to Director of Engineering Services at my workplace.

That idea of **I.A.N** (Interactive Audience Network) took approximately one year of planning and effort to get off the ground. It got off the ground in August 2022. Likewise, I created an app called **C.A.T** (Comments Analysis Tool) that can run reports by sifting through thousands of comments under any social media video telling a content creator what the audience is saying as a group. These led me to start my business, Ideas to Innovation, right in the middle of the pandemic! I published articles in magazines and wrote and published a free e-book on how to create apps without having to learn how to code.

To improve my skills further, I had also joined a Toastmasters Club—Dynamic Speakers—to improve my public speaking. To my delight, I was recently given a leadership role as the president. To top it all off, I completed my doctorate in July 2022 and officially became Dr. Conrad Miller, Dr. B.A, Strategy and Innovation.

None of this would have been possible without God's grace and the loving and supportive people in my life. My mother, Yvonne Harvey, kept encouraging me through all my hard times. My ever-loving better half and partner, Latoya Lobban, supported me throughout my rough times. My dear aunt Maxine Clarke helped me finance my education by providing me with a much-needed loan. I give them all the glory! Everything that I went through made me who I am today: a better person, husband, father and leader.

How can you use challenges to help you become better, more aligned with your truth and build what matters most to you?

What I Learned

Ironically, during the struggles faced, I didn't necessarily become **tougher**. Sure, I became more durable in terms of inner strength, but I actually became more in touch with who I am. I think more of others now than myself; I saw more than ever the importance of friends and family. I have fallen in love with innovation and finding and bringing out the creativity in others.

I regained my drive and my momentum. I share this story not to paint this as a peak of achievement, but to help my readers face one fact. Many times in life, we all have objectives and dreams that sometimes feel like boulders weighing us down underwater. But by reconnecting with ourselves, God, faith in our higher purpose and asking for support from our close ones, anything is possible.

What YOU Can Learn From This

Just like me, what we thought would be a two-month flu has turned out to be an extended pandemic. Whatever challenges you have faced so far in the pandemic or that you will face, you CAN overcome them. Do what I did and . . .

Find your purpose:
What is your reason for doing what you're doing? Once you find your purpose, nothing will be able to stop you. You will find the strength to overcome any obstacle.

Connect with yourself, God, and your close ones:
These are the people who will help support you through tough times. Lean on them for encouragement and inspiration.

Ask for support:

Don't be afraid to ask for help when you need it. We all need a little assistance from time to time.

Never give up on your dreams:

Keep your head up and keep moving forward. You will achieve your goals if you don't give up.

Surround yourself with positivity and Knowledge:

Listen to inspirational stuff on social media, not negativity or conspiracy theories. Energy flows where attention grows. So make sure to be aware of what you place your attention on.

With these practices, I was able to achieve a lot despite the pandemic. The pandemic has been a difficult time for everyone. But it doesn't have to be all doom and gloom. There are ways to find hope in the chaos and turn this negative situation into a positive one. Believe me, you can too. Did you know that between 2020 and 2021, over 5 million people **became millionaires** during the pandemic? That is the meaning of using lemons to make lemonade. So, **don't let the pandemic stop you from achieving your goals. Let it be the reason why you achieve them.** And if you need help along the way, reach out to anyone who can support you—friends, family, coaches and mentors. We are all in this together! If the support you need is related to making your innovative ideas a reality, I would be more than happy to help you achieve your dreams.

I believe that if you follow these tips, you will be able to find hope in the midst of chaos and come out more vital than ever before. Life is a journey; but I have to say had I known these tidbits, I might have been one of those 5 million lemonade makers! **Use challenges as an opportunity to grow and achieve your dreams. Stay positive and keep moving forward! My great-est wish is that you will always find the brighter side of any struggle, any challenge, any pandemic. May you align to your greatest version of yourself!**

Dr. Conrad Miller

Dr. Conrad Miller is an engineer, entrepreneur and innovator. He is the creator of the Interactive Audience Network (I.A.N), a next-generation creator platform for creators and fans. This "Business-Engineer" got the idea to create I.A.N while pursuing his D.B.A. (Doctor of Business Administration) specializing in Strategy and Innovation. His dream is to make life easy for the next generation of content creators, educators, and performers.

Dr. Conrad Miller has also worked with entrepreneurs and innovators to help them develop new and innovative ways to build their technology services. He is an Engineering Services Manager at a power plant in Jamaica, where he oversees the power plant's reliability operations to ensure things run smoothly. He has worked in the business and energy industries for over 20 years and has seen them grow and evolve.

Dr. Miller is also the founder of Ideas to Innovation, a company specializing in turning creative ideas into reality. He has a passion for invention and creativity and is now dedicated to helping others turn their innovative visions into something tangible. He believes innovation is the key to success in today's ever-changing world and works tirelessly to empower others to bring their unique ideas to life.

In the other parts of his life, Dr. "I.A.N" is the father of two and lives with his fiancée, Latoya Lobban, at his home in Jamaica. When he is not working hard on a work or home project, Conrad can be found playing one of his six musical instruments from his collection at home.

Dr. Miller can be contacted by email (**ianetwork2021@gmail.com**) or the following social media handles:

Facebook: Interactive.Audience.Network
TikTok: doctor_i.a.n

Instagram: interactive.audience.network
YouTube: Interactive.Audience.Network
Twitter: @IAN_Interactive
LinkedIn: Ideas To Innovation

SECTION 2:
STEP INTO YOUR POWER AND TRANSFORM

SURVIVING AND THRIVING DURING THE PANDEMIC
BY TRACY TIGHE

Let's start in the present and circle back. I have learned so much during this time in my life. Mother Nature continues to have me look in the reflective waters. I envision swans and lily pads and less often I see salmon in the last smelly stage of life!

As I share the story of my personal journey during the pandemic, I am asking you to think about what are your personal values, and what brings you joy. As you do, I suggest you journal. Be connected with what brings you the quality of life with joy, time spent with loved ones, whatever you need to do in order to live your best life.

My first experience of the pandemic began on the exact cruise ship that was left out at sea in San Francisco Bay a few weeks later. I along with Fempires were on a week's cruise for entrepreneur empowerment. *Fempires is a profitable organization run by a woman that has several revenue streams and has great impact in the community or industry it serves.* One moment I am with this group having the time of my life decked out in boas and sparkle, being an invited group by the ship's captain, and the next thing is I am ill with a virus that led into mid-February.

This created a journey on how to seek knowledge about my new identity. In December of 2019, I had my last teaching job. This was a really fun experience working with a second-grade class from August until December. My teaching job was to educate a group of English language learners. I had been asked to teach in an emergency situation. I agreed to step in and help the class.

We gardened, something I had only done at that precise age with my dad. I recall the carrots we grew the soil, nutrients and the taste of the freshly grown carrot. We went on a field trip which included walking from Napa Valley Language Academy to Connolly Ranch Education Center. "At Connolly Ranch, our mission statement is to instill children of all ages with a deep respect for the environment, a strong understanding of farming and sustainable agriculture, and a love for the natural world." From there, we hiked up Westwood Hills. This is where you can view the students' school and much of the town of Napa. Then we went back to the campus. It was a round trip of four miles including going up and down pretty steep rocky hills.While this was a fun healthy trip, a few children were quite bushed at the end. What I did not share is that years previous I had broken my ankle. I was not going to say "no" to the children having this day of good fun, education and exercise. A parent helped me down the rocky hills. We all survived. The trip was well worth seeing the smiles on these seven- and eight-year-old faces. Little did we know in the coming months, our smiles would be covered up by masks. Children would be on Zoom receiving lessons from their teachers.

At the same time, my identity was transitioning. No longer would I be the teacher in the classroom. I received a pink slip and joined the ranks of the unemployed. The future and uncertainty were ahead of me. In many ways, this created the gift of time, to discover what are one's most important values. Also, as you will see, it was a period of grief and healing. Yet, when God closes one door, we walk through a new time in life.

In early March, I went to visit my mom, who had suffered with first dementia ten years earlier that led to Alzheimer's. She was living her last days of life in a full-time care facility in Florida. Mom was a "Martha Stewart" styled woman, meaning she had lived her life with all of the high-classed style of entertaining, designing, culinary expertise, interior decorating and caring for the sick. She wore the Pink Candy Striper uniform at Overlook Hospital. She enjoyed helping children who needed occupational therapy.

She loved to play golf and was a talented player. Later in life, she took up her love for interior decorating.

Alzheimer's is a frightful disease where one slowly loses all of these skills and talents. It is an ongoing grieving stage for the family and loved ones. My throat chokes up and tears appear reminiscing about our family's experience. The last day I was with Mom, I led her to the little putting green they had set up. We puttered around. Then I took her for a little stroll around the outside perimeter of the building. We sat gazing at the warm tropical Florida sun, holding hands as we giggled a bit. Mom had lost the ability to speak logically.

When she spoke, it was a bit like rain man meaning in rhyme not making much sense. Yet, she had a twinkle in her eye. The days between my arrival and final visit news of the pandemic were quickly changing the greeting protocols at the check-in. On day two, I signed a health form; by the last day, temperatures were being taken off the guests. Shortly, no guests were allowed to visit. I was feeling grateful for making the trip to see my mom for one final week. Individuals who had family members in care facilities know firsthand the pain and raw sorrow of no visitations and the separations and loss of the days and months to follow. Many of us never saw our loved ones again. Thank you first responders for your care. We all have our stories to share.

I am Tracy Ann Tighe, born in New Jersey and having the joys of beginning my life in the flourishing Garden State. Speaking of gardens, I am a late bloomer due to life circumstances and goals, the most important of which is my college education, eventually receiving my Master's in Education in my late 40s. Graduating from Golden Gate University, San Francisco, with a degree in Hospitality Management at the age of 40, I moved to the bountiful Napa Valley. I had been widowed at the ripe age of 36.

In my early stages of living in our valley, I was employed as a tasting room manager for Charles Krug and worked as a seasonal Wine Educator for Robert Mondavi. This enabled me to become familiar with the seasons and harvests of our most beloved fruit of the vine. Lucky me, I enjoyed working with and knowing Peter and Robert, the Mondavi brothers. In time, I became a math teacher for the local schools. At age 42, I met my husband on an online site matchmaker. He is my best friend. We were married two years later in the beautiful setting of Lake Tahoe.

LESSONS MY MOTHER TAUGHT ME CONTINUE TO GUIDE ME THROUGH LIFE

At 36, when I was newly widowed and enrolled at the local junior college studying culinary arts and earning my associate's degree, I was challenged by loss. I share this as my mom taught me valuable lessons. **One was to find a career which helped and served others. Another is when life becomes difficult to find something you love and do it.** I was already in school learning to make Tiramisu including Pon de Sponga, a.k.a. lady fingers, homemade Italian sponge cake, Mascarpone Cream zabaglione and other culinary desserts, fulfilling my lifelong goals. Thus, I remained in school to eventually graduate from Golden Gate University with a BS in hospitality management.

Knowing this lesson when the pandemic hit visiting Mom, I became involved in an online walking group called Women in Motion led by Carla Frank. The goal was to complete a half marathon by November. My first walk began the day I visited Mom. I was barefoot walking the pier at the local Florida Beach. By November at age 60, I completed both a warmup half marathon and the official half marathon. I remember the joy of crossing the finish line, and seeing the cute notes and whimsical pictures Carla had etched on the cool pavement. There were bubbles, gift bags and celebrations. Oh yes, we received medals as well! Carla led all the Zoom walking sessions and weekly "let's get physical" sessions with a group of women including instructions on self care. I found myself going from the couch to the finish line.

During this time, my mom contacted the asymptomatic virus and was removed from her comfortable living space and placed in a ward to be alone so as not to infect others. As one can only imagine, this was a huge time of depression for those who loved her. I found a healthy group, a goal and friends to connect with.

SUCCESS TIP: FIND A GROUP TO FULFILL YOUR HEALTH AND BE INVOLVED IN ONGOING EXERCISE WITH A GOAL IN MIND

In the fall of 2020, I realized I needed to find a new fulfilling activity. This led me to looking at what I'd be doing in the New Year. It was explained by a United States vet that once he was no longer involved with active duty, he experienced an identity crisis. This is the case with many who transition from one career to another. I knew I enjoyed being social while making my husband my priority when it comes to free time. This includes being free when he is off from working, being ready to travel with him, going to concerts, dining, museums, and walking our Border Collie Lexy. This brought on a time of wonder, curiosity and what to do in order to keep me happy and busy. The Brass ring to living my best life in my sixties and beyond.

Sparkles and squirrels have me spinning! During my years of teaching, I missed being with girlfriends. For several years, I have been a fashion enthusiast. During my teens, my favorite magazine was *Cosmopolitan*. Daily fashion included jewelry that sparkles, shoes that fashionably enhance the outfit, hats and hair accessories with feathers and sparkles. Thus, it makes perfect sense for me to love jewelry. When it was time for me to think of new ways to make an income, I learned about working from home on my own terms. Thus, I jumped in with both feet. I had a blast being a business owner and putting on home shows and doing events. During this time, I earned incentive trips to Alaska, Maui and Las Vegas. I formed a sales team of business associates who shared the same interest.

I enjoy boosting the confidence of women who love fashion. This is financially rewarding and comes with freedom from working a 9 to 5 job. I found the home business a way to first make an income after leaving my full-time teaching job and waiting to earn a retirement. Now that I am retired, I use it to boost my income adding to my retirement salary. I love to travel, shop, give to charities and take education classes. Lots of my ongoing education is centered out of an amazing group called Thriving Women in Business, led by Caterina Rando. She offers sales courses based upon pillars including serving, sales, self care, speaking and strategy. One of the highlights is going on bliss retreats.

During the pandemic, it was a challenge of not having home shows and keeping the business afloat. Thus, we were faced with the challenge of doing shows virtually. The solution was to learn to do online shows along with games such as Blingo, etc. to offer something entertaining and fun to others who were missing friends and looking for something to do. On Christmas Eve, my birthday, I offered a birthday Blingo. The purpose was providing a source of entertainment for friends and associates. My friend Tom Overton surprised everyone at the end by playing the ukulele and singing Christmas songs and a few Hanukkah songs—brightening the lives of many.

Super Tip: Embrace Philanthropy. Find charitable groups, individuals and causes that need financial assistance. Offer a Bingo fundraiser. Join Thriving Women in Business (tell them I sent you).

ANOTHER TIP: TRAVEL

I love to travel. The previous year, my husband and I had taken a journey to Ireland. Every Sunday morning, we began our day by listening to Irish music. With this in mind once everyone was wearing masks and following the pandemic protocol we took a road trip to Solana Beach, California. We enjoyed beach-combing and quality time together. The beach is our happy place. We also traveled to Yosemite, Mendocino, Carmel, New York City and Las Vegas. In September of 2021, we traveled to Greece. We were overjoyed when we learned we were upgraded to Trafalgar tour group. We went to Athens, Santorini, and Mykonos, touring the Acropolis, Fira, Oia, black volcanic sand beaches, Paraportiani and more. The tour attendance numbers were quite low and we enjoyed visiting these areas with lower visitor attendance. Lucky us!

Mom had died and I was depressed and sad, unmotivated by my activities I loved including serving women with sparkle. A friend of mine from a different company continued to keep in contact with me. I had been to her home for fashion shows. Quietly, I followed her on social media, enjoying her emails and ways of communication. We had reviewed ways of doing virtual shows as well. Taking note of her professionalism and wit, I was inspired to be a part of the brand we both now represent. One October evening at dinnertime, she called me. When I hung up the phone, my supportive husband inquired as to what the call was about. I told him and then heard him suggest I speak with her. In my mind, I heard my mom's message about when times turn difficult, find something I love and do it. Thus, the idea of doing something new in the upcoming year was appealing.

I said "yes" to becoming an Independent Stylist for an innovative boutique fashion brand. We serve others by bringing style and beauty to women through personalized styling experiences that celebrate each woman's uniqueness. We bring the fashion, fun and shopping experience to homes. We empower women to walk more confidently out their doors each morning. I speak about fashion onstage and at conferences. My advice is find your passion and do it. I joined an organization with strong philanthropic ethics helping girls and women around the world. This brand has an excellent training plan.

Needless to say I have grown, achieved goals and am once again *reinspired not retired.*

Success Tip: Find a service that fulfills your needs. Decide what are your passions, goals, and personal trigger points. Join a home business. FYI I am looking to help others experience the journey. Be sure to seek me out if you like fashion, accessories, independent styling and serving women.

The quaint town of Yountville, heart of the Napa Valley, offers a Golden Ticket to seniors. Yountville has a 9-hole course named Vintner's Golf Club. Weekly golf lessons are offered as part of the program. It was time for me to join the Golden Ticket and take up golf. My goal was to renew my skills and play the course. Being amongst nature, friends and out on the greens feels invigorating. A happy balance between play and work is being a golfer.

SUCCESS TIP: FIND A SPORT YOU LOVE AND GO PLAY!

I like to keep my brain active. Alzheimer's disease and dementia concern me. Fundraising for a cure is something I am active in doing. By participating in the Alzheimer's walk, I feel I am doing my part to raise money for research. My husband and I also volunteer and give to other causes. We are regular volunteers for the Jimmy V Foundation for cancer research.

SUCCESS TIP: VOLUNTEER; GIVE FREELY AND LOVINGLY OF YOUR TIME AND DONATIONS

Are you retired? Do you feel that playing golf, going to lunch, reading a book are all great activities, yet at the same time you feel unfulfilled, lonely or unimportant? I have a solution. Stand tall in your power. Open your own business under a social selling company, one that offers reasons for women to gather and for enjoyment . . . a team where there are members to share, one with an income, charitable purpose, freedom to work when and where you desire. This is another way I am living my best life. I am available for public speaking and recruitment.

By sharing my story for *The Power of You*, I have gained insight into finding the tools to live my best life.

In Summary: During the pandemic we all have stories to share. It is a time of growth. With growth comes healing. We were faced with problem-solving. Collaboration. Building a stronger community. Many, including myself, discovered and/or renewed what is most important to us. We suffered loss and are healing. With the lessons learned, I encourage you to stand in your power.

Tracy Tighe

When the pandemic hit, Tracy transitioned from being retired to being reinspired. This is the story of how she as a teacher transitioned to becoming a skilled personal stylist. She has a MA in education and a BS in hospitality management. She has wonderful people skills and a warm, understanding demeanor. She has transitioned to living her best life in retirement years. In her free time, she loves to travel the world. She is an avid concert goer and loves the beach and her social life. Tracy is passionate about fashion and hospitality. With a combination of both her teaching and hospitality skills, she is a highly-skilled and sought-after brand stylist. She has the knowledge on how you can capsule your wardrobe with the benefits of clearing out your wardrobe clutter and enhancing your style and confidence. She is a highly sought-after speaker.

Tracy travels the country facilitating speaking about living your best life after retirement and earning an income by finding your passion. In addition, she speaks about fashion and accessories with the end goal being to help women find the style that pairs well with their identity, having women finding ways to flatter their bodies, feel good about how they look and feel great in what they wear. Tracy enjoys being a leader and helping women be the CEO in their business. She has the reputation of helping all ages of women. She is married to her husband and best friend. They have two fur babies border collie, Lexy, who loves to leap and catch frisbees. The newest addition is Brixy Napa Valley's Sweetest Cavalier. In *The Power of You*, she speaks about the challenges she was faced with and being reinspired to a new way of living her best life. Let her help you look good and feel great! Contact Tracy for speaking engagements. The best compliment is a referral. Looking for opportunities to serve ladies at their work space with talks about fashion, and life following retirement. Make appointments for styling sessions. These offerings are both in person and virtual.

Email: **Tracy@TracyTighe.com**
Instagram: **https://www.instagram.com/tracy_cabi_image_enthusiast/**
Facebook: **https://www.facebook.com/tracytighethestylist/**
YouTube: **https://www.youtube.com/channel/UC76IqWzjdf0ICeite67M5Bw**
https://linktr.ee/TracyImageEnthusiast
https://www.linkedin.com/in/tracy-tighe-57b3561aa/

TOP 3 CORE VALUES TO THRIVE: COURAGEOUS LEADERSHIP OF A SINGLE MOTHER, DOCTOR, AND SMALL BUSINESS OWNER.
BY DR. RITU "RIA" SINGH, DC, IDE, QME

"Adapt, Improvise, Overcome"
—the unofficial slogan of the US Marine Corps

Have you ever traveled home from a memorable vacation and wished you were still there? The first-morning sip of Parisian Cafe Au Lait, the smell of a freshly baked croissant and the glittery panorama of the City of Lights were the thoughts running through my mind as I sat in the aisle seat of the dimly lit 747 and waited to touch down in San Francisco. My two children and I were returning after spending the holidays in Paris and London and looked forward to making our 2020 New Year's resolutions at home with unbridled fervor for the future.

My daughter was in the midst of 11th grade and was excited about prepping for the event most high schoolers look forward to, the junior prom. My son was in his final year of elementary school and was relishing being one of the older kids on campus before his move to middle school in the fall. As for me, I was putting serious thought into bringing an associate doctor into my chiropractic clinic to help me expand. My daughter was teetering closer to college and the thought of paying hefty college tuition as a single parent was motivation enough to work harder and generate more revenue.

As the kids and I made the arduous trek toward baggage claim, I noticed headlines running across some of the TV monitors mentioning a virus from China that was killing people dead in their tracks. I specifically remember seeing a clip of a Chinese gentleman walking out of a building wearing a dark trench coat and collapsing face down onto the concrete sidewalk and being proclaimed dead. There were similar clips that were being shown throughout the airport which were disturbing. It seemed surreal and almost like a fabricated scene from a sci-fi movie. I was secretly hoping Bruce Willis would show up on screen to prove this was just a trailer from a holiday movie release. As the days went on and we settled into our routines, I began hearing more about this virus which was now outside of China and expected to make its way to the US. I didn't panic as I thought it would surely be contained before hitting US soil. That was a thought I wished had come to fruition.

CORE VALUE #1: CRITICAL THINKING

On the beautiful spring morning of my daughter's 17th birthday, I received an email stating that Alameda County was in lockdown and all business unless deemed essential would not be allowed to operate. I immediately texted colleagues if they had heard of this and if chiropractors were considered essential workers. Days went by and neither our state nor county boards gave firm answers as to whether we could open our offices. I was in a unique situation of being a health care worker and a small business owner. The two groups were ironically shut down yet needed. The buzz going around my colleagues was that this shutdown may be in place for a week or two so we should just consider it a mini vacation and enjoy the time off while the virus spread lessened.

For those couple of weeks, the kids and I followed the social media trends of carbo-loading; baking loaves of bread, pizza from scratch, fresh cookies, and even the famous one - dish tomato feta pasta bake. All was fun until we realized that carbo-loading without exercise to burn it off made for a bloated belly and a sluggish attitude that was content being with its counterpart the couch potato. We shifted to daily walks around the local creek and lake trails. It's during these walks that we laughed the most, appreciated our neighborhood the most, and discussed our fears and concerns the most. Children are sponges and absorb their environment and pick up on the energies of the people they spend their time with.

I recognized in my heart that although I had many uncertainties actively running in my mind about the pandemic, my livelihood, our health, and our safety, my children needed to continue to feel they had a safe bubble where fear was not at the forefront. I suppressed my own feelings of stress and fear in front of them. In retrospect, perhaps it wasn't the healthiest for my mental health to keep my emotions bottled up inside. My priority was to protect and navigate my children through our current reality. I was parenting alone and did not have anyone to lean to for support. I was in mama bear mode.

I began to educate them on the science behind what they were hearing from the media and their peers. I encouraged them to ask questions about what they were hearing and not resort to blind absorption of opinions. I believe true learning comes from critical thinking: The ability to ask the hard questions no one else is asking, to do the research, to come up with conclusions, and to feel okay with decisions regardless of the popular opinion at the moment. Critical thinking develops a characteristic of non-reactive behavior which leads to inner confidence and a platform for discussion devoid of judgment.

CORE VALUE #2: RESILIENCE

When I was a kid, I was obsessed with the show "*Lifestyles of the Rich and Famous* with Robin Leach". I never missed an episode. I was in awe of the luxurious food, homes, vacations, and clothes these seemingly amazing people had at their fingertips. I was curious as to how they reached that level of luxury. I wanted to know everything: where they worked, which college they attended, which investments they made. I was more interested in reading the autobiographies of successful people than reading "Sleeping

Beauty" or "Cinderella" for the 51st time. Two things I knew for certain were that I wanted to be my own boss and I had to graduate with a professional degree. My parents were immigrants and education was considered as crucial as oxygen and water.

Knowing that, I wanted to finish college as fast as I could so I could be my own boss and enjoy my own "champagne wishes and caviar dreams." I hustled. I had college classes in the mornings, evenings and weekends all while working as a teller (that's what we were called in the '90s) in a savings and loan. At 24, I graduated with my Doctorate degree in Chiropractic and opened my own private practice. I commenced my journey armed with zero business experience and an abundance of tenacity sworn to become successful.

Over my 26 years in private practice, I've succumbed to many failures and celebrated glorious successes. Both taught me the power of resilience and that neither highs nor lows last forever. Life is dynamic, and when unexpected change occurs, I am thankful to the Almighty for another experience to grow and reflect upon the essence of resilience: "Adapt, Improvise, Overcome."

Chiropractors became essential workers and I was faced with a choice to go back to my office and treat patients with hardly any personal protective equipment. No masks, no sanitizing equipment, and no gloves. Everything was in short supply and so was my bank account. There was a ghost of a chance for me to support my kids and keep a roof over our heads with the government's minimal pandemic relief. Some colleagues were shutting down their offices permanently and planned to rely on their spouse's income, some decided to move out of the area to avoid paying the exorbitant prices associated with living in the SF Bay Area, and some decided to open up their clinics and start seeing patients again. The first two paths were not an option for me but the third seemed slightly feasible if there was a way to mitigate the risk of transmitting the virus to my children.

After several sleepless nights of writhing with the stress of probably the hardest decision of my life, I prayed to the almighty to guide me in making the correct choice. My tear-ladened eyes asked for a sign, a message, something that would ensure that I moved along the correct path.

CORE VALUE #3: THE HEALING POWER OF TOUCH

Two days later, my answering service began receiving phone calls from patients who wanted appointments. I got the sign that I had prayed for.

I decided to open one day a week to see what the patient flow would look like. With one hot pink handmade cloth mask, a bottle of Lysol spray, and food-serving gloves, I was ready to see my first patient. I allowed one patient into the office at a time after all tables and equipment were cleaned from the previous patient. I continued to get more calls from patients and the one day a week quickly became four.

Nearly every patient had the same complaints: neck pain, back pain, shoulder pain; and headaches. Working from home sounded like an amazing scenario but it had its drawbacks, lack of rest breaks and poor ergonomics. Using a laptop in bed, on the sofa, or on the kitchen counter wasn't conducive to good spinal health and relaxed muscles. There is an entire industry designed to evaluate office workers and their postures so as to avoid workplace injuries and fatigue. At home, there was no such guidance. Whether it was for ergonomics or dress code, many were business on top and party on the bottom. In other words, professional tops with PJ's or shorts as bottoms. It was the new normal, and if you are in comfy clothes then it's easier to contort into less desirable working postures.

Science has long discovered that disruption in routine causes mental stress which leads to physical pain. Being able to give or receive a hug or shake somebody's hand was beginning to feel like a forgotten treasure. Patients were afraid to visit hospitals and were frustrated with telemedicine, but were willing to come into my office so they could be seen, heard; and touched.

Chiropractors have long understood the healing power of touch. Our human bodies are designed for physical contact and live human engagement.

Every patient who left my office felt immediate relief, no drugs, no surgery, just the brass tacks of human healing. When I placed my hands on a patient, I felt no fear, no resistance, no hesitation; only the power of one human being connecting with another to help remove their pain and suffering. I had never worked longer hours nor seen as many patients in my entire career. My body was tired yet my soul was energized. I was satiated.

My core values are what enabled me to thrive. Critical thinking, resilience, and the healing power of touch can help navigate the twists and turns of life's path so we may ultimately reach the brighter side even of the pandemic.

This book is dedicated to the tender souls that brought
life to my dreams, Chaiya and Caden.
I love you.

Dr. Ritu "Ria" Singh, DC, IDE, QME

Dr. Ritu "Ria" Singh, DC, IDE, QME has been a practicing chiropractor for 26 years and is a native of the San Francisco Bay Area. She is the founder of Singh Chiropractic and Massage Clinic in Fremont, California. Her mission is to provide a whole-body approach to pain relief and wellness by educating her patients on preventive care, not reactive care.

Dr. Singh received the distinguished honor of being elected into the National Registry of Top Doctors in America under 30. She was also voted one of the Top 100 Women Doctors in the US.

Dr. Singh is a Qualified Medical Evaluator and Independent Disability Evaluator. She serves as Vice President on the Board of Directors for the Alameda County Chiropractic Association. She is nationally and state board certified and a member of the California Society for Industrial Medicine and Surgery and the California Chiropractic Association.

Dr. Singh has been invited as a guest speaker on talk shows to speak on her expertise. She has also hosted her own radio talk shows to discuss various health topics.

Being in private practice for over two decades has allowed Dr. Singh to diagnose and treat many patients with muscular, spinal, and nerve - related problems with great success. She has local and international patients who visit her for treatment.

Of all her many accomplishments, Dr. Singh's proudest moments come from being a mother.

"The doctor of the future will give no medicine, but will interest his (or her) patients in the care of the human frame, in diet, and in the cause and prevention of disease." -Thomas Edison

Website: **www.YourFremontChiropractor.com**
Email: **dr.riasingh@gmail.com**
Instagram: **@dr.riasingh**
Twitter: **@DrRiaSingh**
Facebook: Dr. Singh Chiropractic & Massage Clinic
LinkedIn: Dr. Ritu "Ria" Singh, DC, IDE, QME

A LESSON IN FAITH AND TRUST
BY SEEMA GIRI

"It was the best of times, it was the worst of times, it was the age of wisdom, it was the age of foolishness, it was the epoch of belief, it was the epoch of incredulity, it was the season of light, it was the season of darkness, it was the spring of hope, it was the winter of despair."
—Charles Dickens, A Tale of Two Cities

That is how I can describe the last two years of the global pandemic. For the first time, I could empathize with the soldiers and their families. It was almost a first-hand experience of what war must feel like for them. The only difference is that they chose to embrace uncertainty, whereas the pandemic was sprung on all of us. Perhaps there is still some level of control in the war. Nonetheless, of course there is no comparison.

The last two years have been a roller coaster of fear, courage, faith, trust and uncertainties for those of us in personal development trying to let go of control, certainty and learning to go with the flow. Well, this just helped us overcome all we needed to overnight. At an instant, we had to let go of life as we knew it. For better or for worse, time would tell.

2020 especially taught me at even deeper level to have Faith in God but also to have faith and trust in myself and that it's okay to not have everything planned out and known. I learned to completely give in to my intuition and instincts of what I needed to do rather than giving in to others, relying on my resiliency, resources and my ability to hold space for others in uncertain times. Think about it: at some point in life, we all have gone through our own personal pandemic. We have had our own personal times of uncertainties for decades.

I realized that I had to step up my game to support two families across the oceans while maintaining my own sanity. This is how I learned to have unconditional faith in GOD, universe and myself. See if you can identify the brighter side of my journey along the way.

When the news broke out about the unknown virus that was causing a chaos, then mostly in China, I was preparing for my trip to New Delhi, India, to visit my sister-in-law battling breast cancer. Every news channel was talking about the virus making its way around the world. I didn't give it much of a thought as viruses had been detected many times before and were under control fairly quickly. It's middle of December 2019; as the weeks passed, the news reports got worse.

My family and I started to get really concerned about me travelling at this time. The concern turned into worry when several incidents occurred within a day.

First, I couldn't find my passport. I finally did after hours of ransacking my home, to only find out that my passport has expired. After an hour of negative self-talk and feeling this is a definite sign that I shouldn't travel, I got into my resourcefulness state by breathing, focused on the breath and became grounded quickly. I found a company in San Francisco that does same day passport renewal and they had availability the next day. Yes! This was meant to be, I am flying to India!

I did a mini celebration in my heart. The icing on the cake was that my daughter Ashima did not have any classes or other commitments on that day. Within the chaos, we were able to continue our tradition of spending quality time together before I traveled anywhere.

The drive to San Francisco was gorgeous with a light blanket of fog rolling in with us. We were going to be tourists for the day. After we dropped off my passport, our adventure as the local tourists began. We first went to the house where a popular TV sitcom was filmed in the '90s, *Full House*. I watched the show as a young adult and now my kids watched it too. That was followed by the famous crooked lane, a walk across the infamous Golden Gate Bridge, lunch, and the ocean beach. It was a picture-perfect day.

As we approached the end of our day, we stopped to fuel up our car for our ride home after picking up the passport. Just as I finished pumping the gas and as I closed the driver side door, two men in front of our car started yelling at each other, breaking into a physical fight. Ashima and I were so scared, we froze. There was a crowd starting to gather. Both of us looked at each other, then scrambled to grab our phones to call the police, but our phones would not unlock. Just then, both men fell onto the hood of our SUV. I couldn't move the car or maneuver it in any way to get out because of the car lines behind us anxiously waiting for their turn. I would have expected them to stop with incessant honking going on.

Luckily, one of the men was able to break loose, get in his car and leave just before the cops arrived. This opened up space for us to leave too. Once we reached the passport office, we carefully got out of the car, ran to each other and hugged, making sure the other was okay.

Now I am beginning to think these are definitely the signs from the Universe. In that instant, Gabby Bernstein came to mind with her book *The Universe Has Your Back*. Okay, Gabby, what is the universe telling me? I need it in black and white, please. I have been on my spiritual journey for some time now but when it comes to myself, it takes me a while to understand. It's so much easier for me to translate the messages for others.

If this was not enough, we encountered a hit-and-run on the ride home. This was the fourth warning sign when our GPS rerouted the direction to a different way than the route that we would normally go. I didn't give it much thought since it was the evening rush hour. I was more than happy to save time with a faster route.

We were at a traffic light in Oakland and I noticed an old blue sports car over my right shoulder. I was compelled to slightly turn my head and look. I couldn't articulate it but there was something odd about the driver. As the light turned green, we proceeded to move forward going straight, but this old blue car turned slightly left rather than going straight, hit the front bumper of our car, swerved right and sped away. By the time I realized what happened, I reached out to grab my phone to take a picture of the license plate, the next thing I feel is that we are chasing the old blue car. Shocked, I looked at Ashima, giving her a look of "are you out of your mind?" She said, "There is not going to be a hit-and-run on my watch." I took several pictures but all were unclear. She quickly pulled over to the side and said it wasn't worth it, we are alone in Oakland in the evening time. I was so proud of her presence of mind and maturity. In the midst of this craziness, I managed to have a proud mommy moment. We still reported it to the police over the phone. Luckily, there was no damage to the car or to either one of us. We were just shaken up. We sat in the car for 10 minutes before resuming our drive home, normalizing our breathing and mind. Ashima and I escaped a near-fatal accident. I was immensely grateful for the amazing blessing that it was only a scare and minor inconvenience in our day.

As we drove home, I looked up at the sky to let the Universe know it had my full attention, letting it know I am alert and focused. The whole way, I was trying to make sense of the day, and rationalize the sequence of events to make my human mind understand the essence of the message. I had never been more perplexed in my life. We made it home safe and sound in one piece. Coming home never felt so exhilarating.

My family said, "Let's not take a risk; we have never experienced this before where so many incidents happened in ONE day. Let's not take a chance. There couldn't be a clearer sign."

I called my sister-in-law in Delhi to let her know that it's better for me to not come at this time. Let's wait to see how the virus situation is and the aftereffects of the signs I received. But I didn't cancel my ticket . . . yet!

I didn't feel settled though with this decision. It didn't feel complete to me. I decided to sleep on it. As I lay in bed trying to fall asleep, like a detective, I was recounting the day's events looking for some more clues.

The next morning when I woke up, I thought to myself out of all the possibilities that can happen what would be that one scenario that would make me feel the worst for the rest of my life? The answer was very clear: the possibilities of not being able to share what's in my heart with my sister-in-law, of missing the opportunity to help her work through some difficult emotional decisions that wasn't working well sorting through over the phone. It required the personal touch to help her gain clarity and sort through her fears of letting go and accepting that the end was getting closer. At this point, my pain, suffering and inconvenience didn't matter because I felt it was nothing compared to what she was going through. I had to go. I realize today that this was not a selfless act but a selfish one. I needed to go for me.

I had faith in God that if I am making these decisions, taking these steps, then my team of God (Lord Shiva) and Goddesses (The Trio Goddesses Lakshmi, Durga and Saraswathi) that I believe in will be there to see me through it.

My family was on board with me. I changed my flight to an almost nonstop flight that had a thirteen-hour layover in New Jersey. I took this opportunity to rent a car and visit family friends. I said my goodbyes like I always do when I travel: how much I adore them, what I love the most about them and how deeply I love them in case these are the last words they hear from me.

The six weeks there was an amazing experience. It was exactly what the heart needed for all of us. I was able to be in service not only to my sister-in-law but to my nephew, niece and brother-in-law. I was a welcomed distraction from their routine. Most importantly they were able to rest.

My sister-in-law and I had our heartwarming and heart-wrenching conversations. Although the life expectancy was much shorter than what we wanted, she felt that she had lived a full life. We relived our life-defining moments that we had together in the ten years that I lived in India. This trip from the beginning was filled with difficult choices and decisions. The day that I was to return home, March 10th, my sister-in-law was in extreme pain and had to be hospitalized. I couldn't leave the family in this situation. We held our breath waiting for the call from the hospital. We had reached the stage that we could get any news. I extended my ticket for another week. Next day, she came home and the world announced a complete shutdown. All modes of transportation out of the country were closed.

Shutdown was announced indefinitely. No one could go out to the office or anywhere except for the basic groceries.

I remember standing there in disbelief completely shocked, staring at the television screen. The faces of my husband, daughter, son and dog flashed by. Every day and all day, we were glued to the TV for the latest info. It was crazy. After two weeks I decided, I am only going to watch the news twice a day: in the morning and evening. In between, if there was any news that would affect me someone would call.

I knew how I reacted would make a difference on how my families would react. I was in the middle of my first book production, *Break Free to Stand in Your Power*. I was leading 17 amazing entrepreneurs, all first-time authors. I had to step up and truly step into my power to lead this book to success.

I decided to take control of what I could. I pulled out my coaching wisdom on wellness, self-care and mindset. I did a fact check. The reality was that in the time of uncertainty, I had certainty that all my loved ones were safe and healthy with full resources available to them. We all had comfortable shelter with plenty of space to be where we are not on top of each other. In the US, we had an amazing beautiful backyard where my kids, husband and our dog Cartie could enjoy. In India, we had a balcony. Most important of all, we had this amazing technology, the internet; it was a household phenomenon that everyone could afford. Everyone had it. I could talk to Upendra, Aman and Ashima for hours; I could see them through video calls for free. What a blessing.

The biggest blessing was that I had a business that I could run from anywhere. So why not embrace it? I started enrolling people in my next two books simultaneously: *Break Free to Peace, Love & Unity* and *Break Free to Health and Vitality*. These two books were inspired by events and incidents we were experiencing during the pandemic.

To keep our mind sharp and body moving, our daily routine was meditation and yoga in the morning, then a healthy breakfast, then watch the news. Throughout the day, we would walk in the hallway. I had set times to connect with my US family, clients and friends. I continued business as usual. We were on track with our author interviews for my podcast *Break Free to Brilliance*.

I made sure that we all had a chance to share what we were feeling. Our emotions were jumping all over. One moment we had full composure and faith, the next moment we were frightened. Luckily, we were experiencing this at different times. We had to surrender to what was happening. We had to go with the flow.

We exercised creativity by experimenting in the kitchen with new recipes that we never made. We created a schedule of cooking, cleaning and doing dishes. For the first time, we were grateful to have these chores to keep us busy.

After three weeks, it seemed apparent that the lockdown was going to go for some time. My children were now beginning to say, "Mom, find a way to come home. We have no idea how long it's going to be or what will happen." My sister-in-law was so scared she wanted me to wait longer. These were the moments I had to stand my ground to make my own decisions. I didn't want to make it emotionally by what anyone was saying and later say because of so-and-so I made a decision that didn't work out. If a decision could possibly end my life, it had to be mine. I needed that for me and for others so they don't feel the guilt.

This was an extremely difficult thing for me to do, to truly stand in my power. All my life decisions were either made for me or I was always compromising and accommodating. It felt like walking through an endless thick pile of mud of deciding my next perfect move. I had to trust my instincts.

I became resourceful. I began to think outside the box and started to look at what facilities do I have in India being a US citizen. I reached out to the embassy and discovered that US was beginning to operate special flights, airlifts to take the US citizens home. I completed the form. I had to be very vigilant and be ready to leave at any moment. I could only have one bag. I was checking my email every 10 minutes to make sure that I don't miss the window of opportunity to respond. I finally got my call date, April 12, 2020. I could possibly make it home in time for my birthday and can be done with my quarantine in time for my daughter's birthday. It was a big relief for all of us. My sister-in-law and I could resume celebrating our birthdays together once again. Hers was on the 13th and mine on the 14th of April.

Then came another major decision; this was the most difficult one of all. We were informed that due to limited flights and in an effort to help everyone get home they could not practice social distancing. There were no virus tests at that time except for making sure that we don't have a cold, cough and fever. They checked for fever at the airport. This meant that there could be a high probability of getting infected. Can I take that risk of potentially exposing my family to this? My children had their whole lives ahead of them. Do I go or stay? Ugh, I felt nauseated by the thought. I felt like I was intentionally walking through a minefield not knowing which step will cause the explosion. I surrendered this to a power beyond me—GOD. I prayed for a few days until I got the assurance that I should go. My family knew of the potential consequences for which they were willing to accept.

April 12th: finally the day to leave came. I was so grateful to have the extra time with my sister-in-law and her family. The bond and connection exponentially became stronger. I never thought in my wildest imagination that I would see the streets of Delhi empty. Complete silence! Not a soul on the road. There was only one other car that I saw on the 45-minute ride to the airport.

I checked in at the Indira Gandhi International Airport and my name was not on the list. I was asked to stay on standby, they will try to accommodate me once everyone on the list has checked in. After 6 hours of waiting, I was notified that I could get on this flight. I was getting really good at navigating my internal roller coaster of emotions. I was quite a sight to look at with all the protection I had on: double masks, silk scarf to cover my head, triple gloves in case there was a tear in any of them.

Once I boarded the plane, it looked like a full normal flight like any other time. Besides blocking of some seats, we were all sitting next to each other. I sank into my seat and finally exhaled with relief. I was on my way home. My next challenge was on how to avoid the bathroom for the next 16 hours.

This was the longest 16 hours of my life but it finally came to an end. I could finally see my family's faces. As I walked through the San Francisco International Airport, the only people there were those that came on the flight. There was one coffee place open thankfully.

Upen and Ashima came in two separate cars so that I could be alone in the car. I had to use all the power I had within me to not run and hug and kiss both of them. We rejoiced in being together again from a distance and proceeded on the drive home. We talked over the phone.

Finally, I arrived at my home sweet home. My family, my home and our dog were a sight for sore eyes. I never felt more lucky, blessed and blissful than I did at this moment.

I directly went to my bedroom for the next 14 days of quarantine. These 14 days were nerve-wracking. I thought with the jet lag it would be easier. I didn't have to worry about getting up by a certain time or prepare meals. I had the shortest jet lag ever. Every pain, sneeze, sniffle, headache and cough made everyone wonder if I had the virus. Every hour I was being asked, "How do you feel?" It was crazy.

I relied on my routines of meditation and yoga while completing the next steps of the book production to get me through this time. I was doing my daily lives on Facebook sharing my quarantine journey. I looked forward to the times of the fireside chat style we had when each member would come to spend time with me. They were in the hallway and I was as far back as possible in my room. And then my connection time with my family in Delhi.

Blessings were all around me and my loved ones. Blessings to all.

It truly was the worst of times and the best of times. Because I tuned out some of the noise, relied on my wisdom, strength and fully stepped into my power, the brighter side for me was that I was able to build a stronger relationship with myself. I could trust myself no matter what.

I have this amazing ability to hold space for people for their own trans-formational journey even though I was going through a tough time. I could put that aside at the most critical time and support others.

My business grew in an area that I had not expected or planned for. Most importantly, I was able to be of service to thousands of people at a time that was needed the most. Through my amazing authors, we were able to show the light of hope, possibilities and miracles.

So, what was the message the Universe was giving me? I chose to receive the message that any unexpected turn can occur on this journey that is life. Sometimes the signs are not to stop with your journey but to step into it despite what is happening with courage and caution. Some days are more eventful than others. No matter what comes my way, I can handle it even alone. I always get support from amazing people around me. I have the wisdom, experience, knowledge and I am more present in the moment. I realized that I have been preparing all my life for what each moment brings to me. I got this.

I believe the way I approached each situation and my work was spiritual. I made sure that every interaction I had come from a place of love and understanding. I was just as compassionate to myself as I was to others and I did some activity daily that brought me joy. I intentionally worked on keeping my vibration high.

What are your thoughts?

You my friend, YOU got this too!

The best advice I can give you to thrive in uncertain times are to:

1. **Embrace** mindfulness. Breathe, remember to pause and breathe. The breath will always calm you and ground you. Consciously choose your thoughts.
2. **Expand** compassion and kindness to yourself as you would do for a friend.
3. **Evaluate** the situation. Do fact checks when faced with uncertainty. There are always some things that you are still in control of.
4. **Extend** your strength, courage and wisdom to others who are struggling.

5. **Focus** on the 3 M's: your Mission, Mindset and Movement. Look at what you need to get through in the short term and long term. Meditation and Movement are crucial to manage emotions, anxiety and stress. They stimulate critical thinking and creative possibilities.

6. **Stay connected** to your inner circle.

I want to leave you with this. You are here to share your gifts. The best way to do that is to live your life full out. Live today; don't wait for the perfect time. The perfect time to do what you want is NOW. Now is all that we have!

Seema Giri

Seema Giri is a four-time #1 international bestselling and award-winning author, book-writing mentor, public speaker, and storyteller with a 30-year career in coaching and mentoring, having impacted the lives of over 100,000 leaders and entrepreneurs from diverse backgrounds. As a project management expert, she has PMP® (Project Management Professional) and DASSM (Disciplined Agile Senior Scrum Master) certifications. Seema has received multiple commendations as a Toastmasters public speaker including the Distinguished Toastmaster Award. She is a certified Alternative Medicine practitioner with expertise in Reiki Master and advanced certifications in Pranic Healing. Through the years, Seema has been featured in international publications including *Times of India, Hindustan Times,* and *Dainik Jagran.* She is also one of the top quoted professionals on US media outlets such as ABC, NBC, and CBS. Recently, she has been featured in online publications such as *Thrive Global* and *Authority Magazine.*

Seema gained expertise in various fields for decades, but her core mission remains the same—to empower women to take action in their own lives. She serves this mission through her storytelling platform, Shine Your Brilliance as an Author Program through which she offers mentorship to leaders and entrepreneurs to turn their inspiring transformational stories into individual books or chapters in multi-author books. She publishes their stories in anthologies that have all become #1 international bestsellers as well as their own book.

Seema was inspired to take on this mission after co-authoring the best-selling book *The Authorities* with New York Times Bestselling authors Dr. John Gray (*Men Are From Mars, Women Are From Venus*), Marci Shimoff (*Happiness for No Reason*) and Raymond Aaron (*Double Your Income Doing What You Love*). In the book, she shared her journey of suffering from and rising above autoimmune disease. For years, doctors told her that she was to be bedridden for the rest of her life. Seema refused to accept their diagnosis and found a way for her to heal and become a successful entrepreneur, wife, and mother. When it was released, so many people reached out saying they learned so much from her journey, either as someone with the same condition or having a loved one with a similar affliction. The experience made her realize how important it is to share our stories—to inspire better understanding among one another and serve as motivation for others to take charge of their lives.

Seema has published four anthologies, all during the pandemic: *Break Free to Stand in Your Power*; *Break Free to Peace, Love, and Unity*; *The Art of Leadership*; and *Break Free to Health and Vitality*. All the anthologies feature leaders and entrepreneurs who share their inspiring personal stories of growth. Becoming published authors has helped these experts gain recognition in their respective fields. It has likewise become a key tool for people to be inspired and stay positive and optimistic of what the future holds.

Shine Your Brilliance Facebook group: **https://www.facebook.com/groups/shineyourbrilliance**
Facebook Page: **https://facebook.com/seemagiri.breakfree/**
LinkedIn: **https://www.linkedin.com/in/BreakFreetoBrilliance**
Instagram: **https://www.instagram.com/giriseema1**
YouTube: **http://bit.ly/BreakFree2BrillianceChannel**
Podcast: **https://www.seema.vip**
Author Opportunities: **https://www.seema.vip**

TRACES OF GRACE
BY CHWEN LIM

"Getting started is the hardest part, this is one of the reasons people don't finish their book," so said Seema Giri, my book coach.

So true! When you look at a glass with water half-filled, do you complain that why only half a glass or you are thankful as you have half a glassful of water to drink?

The past three years went on like a blink of eyes. Sometimes, I lost count, I wondered what had happened to 2019, 2020, 2021. Now that we are in 2022 going to 2023...where has the time been? I had to remind myself the virus started in 2019.

There were so many happenings globally and locally, even personally. When I look at memory lane—I am glad that I was able to see traces of grace despite the many challenges... Blessings in disguise?!!

THINGS I CELEBRATE

In November 2018, after my annual physical examination, I was called to meet up with an endocrinologist and was informed that I had "autoimmune system disorders- Hyperthyroidism (Grave's disease). Doctor confidently said that she could treat me with prescription drugs, but I would probably gain weight and require regular blood tests. If all things went on well, I would be able to kick off the medication after two years; Otherwise, I would need to go for surgery and take medication for my whole life.

When I started the medications and saw the weight gain in me, it was scary and depressing; I had to wear loose clothing as if I was pregnant. Thankfully it was during this period when all meetings went online, I didn't have to attend a meeting in person, but only to show my head and neck on zoom meetings. Some friends encouraged me to discuss with my doctor to integrate functional nutritional products and lifestyle changes. Our goal is to stop the medications within two years. With their supervision, I obediently took prescription drugs and nutraceutical supplements concurrently, together with a lifestyle program and weekly acupuncture. Truly in 2021, my endocrinologist wrote to me that I could stop taking the prescription drugs.

Hence, I was glad that my Grave's disease was being controlled and I could do my meetings online without fail despite my embarrassing weight gain.

Personal Growth

"If you do not advance, you will retreat" (不進則退)
—*Chinese idioms*

Other things to celebrate include my participation in two anthologies: "Art of Leadership" and "Art of Connection- 365 days of networking."

Thanks to Seema's guidance, I was able to contribute a chapter about my growth from a Reluctant leader to someone who is willing to pick up the baton. It was a great self-discovery journey. And I learned what it was like to work with a book coach and be attentive to different timelines, to submit drafts, to review and edit my writing. Then came the very interesting book launch on Amazon, followed by the summit, all scheduled and planned if you work with a book coach & her publishing team. I strongly recommend that new book authors start with that route to get a taste of book writing and publishing.

Right after I submitted my writing to Seema, I received a call from the publisher of the "Art of Connection- 365 days of networking." My coach, Jill Lublin, recommended them to reach out to me as she knows that I have been networking a lot during this period. So, I said, "Yes!" (that's what I learned from Jill) and started to draft my message. I chose the date, Feb 26, to commemorate my late father, who brought me to various networking events to broaden my circle when I was young. These were not in my plan before, but worth celebrating as I pick on the opportunities to step out of my comfort zone. Perfection cannot be done without action. One can plan for a long time, but sometimes we just need to put it into action.

ONLINE NETWORKING

It was during this time that I decided to join online networking events to promote my web business. I have been helping SMEs build their websites for more than 15 years. From word of mouth to referrals from cold market. I saw a tendency for my clients to want to move their products and services online. We worked with our tech support/customer service day and night. So glad that I partnered with this IT/Web development company in Las Vegas since 2005, I love that they are always there to support me and my clients 24/7, with four different languages, namely: English, Spanish, Mandarin, and Cantonese. They are my lifeline whenever my client needs help. I am especially in debt to them during this challenging time. "Do you have a system?" "What will happen if you are not there in your business?" these words by Michael Gerber kept ringing in my ears whenever I indulged in many projects. I love to work and am very involved in my client's projects. My husband always likes to challenge me if I have a "system" to truly let myself to rest or to be duplicated. When you look at the word "system," can you see: Save yourself from stress, time, energy, and money?! So true right?!

During this challenging time, I can say that my investment in this partnership reaped rewards. I was so glad that my tech support was there to help and support my many clients with their online needs. We heard many horror stories... when programmers were hard to be found, many were being laid off or sick, some webmasters or engineers even passed away due to the virus. I am thankful that no matter what happens, I know the company I partnered with will have tech support to help me and my clients. I could enjoy the assurance in peace.

I Know What I Do Not Know

I was brave enough to hire coaches, first about publicity. I initially thought that it was a class where I can learn about publishing in the USA. During the pandemic, a few of us gathered and wanted to do something that can support non-profit with a subscription base project, so I bravely enrolled in a training program to learn about the process. Guess what? I misread the course syllabus and regretted after I attended the first class. I talked to the coach and later found that the following sessions will help me walk out of my comfort zone with my "publicity" speech; I found myself enrolling in the two days boot camp and eventually the six weeks programs. My coach, Jill Lublin, has great network, she could connect us with many of her broadcasting networks. I learned a lot from her. Today, I continue to refer people to her and attend some of her online events.

As an introvert, I was always shy to speak to many people I didn't know. I decided to attend Kristy Roger's Business Friend online events to see what other business owners are doing during this period. As a BNI alumni, I was trained to deliver my informercial in 30 sec. However, with this group, I had to answer a few questions about myself and a few about my business every week. The atmosphere was cozy, and those who attended were from different industries, mostly women. It was a great start for me as the cost was affordable. Surprisingly, I had a few clients from that group which elevated my influence and confidence.

From there, I know someone who attended BNI, a networking group which I leveraged 15 years ago when my sons were in kindergarten. I was able to build my web business with BNI for 9 years, but I had to freeze for 5 years due to extensive traveling. I know the impact of joining BNI, the effective referral system and the role of responsibilities if you are determined to commit. Every business entrepreneur needs an accountability group and I know I need one too. I visited a few times and I decided to re-join BNI. The decision was right at that time, the new chapter I joined was very creative and every meeting was indeed entertaining, powerful and result-producing. I had a few referrals from that group too. BNI has changed a lot since my last membership. They have online platforms that track and provide support to BNI members. During this pandemic period, those were very crucial and beneficial for me. I must prepare my informercial every week and my 10 mins presentation per quarter; I got to do 1-1 with many aspiring entrepreneurs. We build strong rapport and relationships so that we can provide better referrals.

When I looked at the three big calendars that I bought during those few years, the pages were filled with notes and appointments, being a visual person, I like to see my schedule at a glance and then down to weekly, daily, and hourly. I learned to prioritize my 1-1 meetings, so much so that I need time to rest and eat; I realized I became FOMO (Fear of Missing Out). Online learning had become so convenient that I can do meetings back-to-back in my casual wear (waist down), save time, save gas, save dressing, and make-up time. It was an interesting phenomenon.

Some complained about not having to meet in person, I truly enjoyed it.

As a web designer, I got to meet my clients online (face to face). I got to show them our solutions and platforms with our portfolios; I enjoy looking at those sites they like or dislike. It helped to streamline my SOP. I could address my clients' needs better. Most importantly, my clients could chat with me anytime, within reach of their computer or phone via zoom. This is one of the brighter sides of the pandemic for me, as everyone is ready and prepared to go online, regardless of their age and tech skill. I was grateful that during the pandemic, I was able to receive a few awards from my company, including "Certified Webcenter Trainer of the year 2019, 2021," and the recent one, "Amplify Sales Contest Top Winner," I received this award in August 2022.

Virtual Is Fine

I recalled those days when we were on zoom but refused to show our face (video turned off due to shyness). Today, not only that we want to show our faces we also work on having a nice virtual background, always ready to celebrate or to match a certain theme. We could have online birthday partis, online virtual camps, online game nights, even our Church services were online. Looking at the elderly trying their best to learn to go online —one could only say

"All will be good" ("the boat will naturally go straight when it touches the bridge" — Chinese idioms).

Family Time Gained

During the pandemic, I had to stop all traveling. My husband always wished that I could just stay home, do the cooking, clean the house and be with him. These two years of pandemic served his wishes. We both worked from home, one of our sons came back to live with us and studied online due to the lockdown of his expensive private school. Only the elder son was staying in San Diego as he worked for CRU as a full-time missionary.

We had lots of quality family time together. We baked, we cooked, we tried different cuisine, we played board games, we facetimed the other son in SoCal, we prayed and had bread-breaking holy communion together, we discussed a lot of interesting topics. I enjoyed seeing my sons grow to be more mature, getting ready to find their life partners. It was rewarding to be home so much and get to learn new technology from these Z generations.

When the bakery stores were closed due to lockdown, we started to crave for bread. But the flour was hard to get, yeast too was expensive. However, I enjoyed making bread with our younger son. My bread would look good, but it was hard like a stone, couldn't be eaten, thus ended up in the trash bin. I couldn't understand, I tried so many times, I made it by following the instruction carefully; However, my son's way of making bread was more of "estimation," a spoonful of this, a dash of that, and his bread raised nicely and tasted good. We baked till late night until my husband was awakened by the wonderful smell from our kitchen.

FROM BRICK AND MORTAR TO CLICK AND ORDER

Then we tried online shopping when brick and mortar stores were shut down. From clothing to accessories to groceries (usually we don't buy fresh groceries online), those were the things we tried. Sometimes, one would get mad as the products that came were not what we wanted. I remembered paying $7.50+ tax and shipping for a white surgical mask (the one we all wear now) back then from a costume store. I was very angry when I received the mask, wanted to return but what could you do when the whole world needed masks?

We saw the convenience of shopping online, safe, no need to keep any distance, no need to worry much except to clean your package when it arrives. No wonder the online marketplace was doing so well, as they met the needs of consumer, they are essential! Thanks to my past investment in an online marketplace, we were able to stay actively growing during the pandemic.

SHARING STORIES VIA MEDIA

In fact, during the pandemic, I was invited to produce video and record my testimonies of how the tragic accident of my mom and brother led us to knowing Christ. The video testimony was filmed by my husband and edited by my younger son, Hanzen, while the cartoon version was my debut piece from the class with instructor Stephen Wong. How I ended up learning from him was a blessing too. I lost my talented designer friend, Kasi, during the Pandemic and his wife later created a series of cartoon animations to commemorate him, I was curious and asked to learn from her instructor. As a result, I created my stories too. Thanks to Zoom technology and the urge to reach out to more people, I was willing to step out of my comfort zone. Now, the videos are used in different media to share God's amazing work.

The pandemic period is the best time, forcing all people to go online and see that online service/tools are crucial. Many were being empowered to breakthrough from their comfort zones, becoming a better equipped person.

"Hey, you are positive again?!!" familiar text by my husband whenever he knew anyone tested positive. As I was writing, he tested positive too, now he had to say, "I joined the positive gang too!"

"When we change the way we see things, the things we see start to change."

Chwen Lim

Chwen Lim is passionate about graphic design and enjoys coaching small and medium-sized businesses through creating online branding to tell the story of their products and services on the web. Chwen earned her Honors degree in Graphic Design from Central Saint Martins—University of the Arts London and her postgraduate teaching diploma from Nanyang Technological University, Singapore.

After Chwen moved to California with her husband and two sons, she continued her education at West Valley College and learned web design.

She became a mentor to other students in the program and created a solid network of new friends and business contacts.

In 2005, Chwen joined maWebCenters® and became a Certified WebCenter Trainer in 2007. Collaborating with the website building platform helped her provide intuitive website designs her clients could easily update independently. Chwen has been recognized for her leadership and training abilities, earning both the WebCenter Trainer of The Year three times and multiple Webcenter Challenge Awards, another one in 2022 "Amplify Sales Contest."

Chwen has traveled extensively throughout Asia for her online business and also to ensure her late artist father's work is professionally curated and documented. She worked closely with museum curators, art gallery owners and collectors to educate future generations on South East Asia art history. Before his passing in 2008, Chwen helped her father put together the giant public mural art piece, "Let the Show begin," in Singapore's underground train station, "Esplande station."

Painting in the studio with her young and adult students is a favorite way for Chwen to reconnect with her artistic roots. She also conducts annual creative summer programs for children and coaches teachers. She is actively involved with community and business networking as a member of organizations like Business Network International (BNI) and is currently a member of Cupertino Rotary, USA

Linkedin: **https://www.linkedin.com/in/chwenlim/**
Facebook: **https://www.facebook.com/chwenlim**

PANDEMIC FROM A POLICE LENS
BY DR. G.K. GOSWAMI IPS

In January 2022, I heard about the pandemic said to be originated in China and slowly spreading across countries as an unprecedented pandemic. Slowly, disease creeped in India, where I live. The horror of the pandemic virus started panicking people around, posing humongous challenge to the Indian Health Care system as well administrative setup.

The first case was identified on January 30, 2020, in Kerala to a student returned to India from Wuhan—the epicenter of the virus—in China. (Source: *India Today*, 30 January 2020) Administrative machinery, including police, came to motion to face this exceptional threat to human life. By mid-March 2020, 500 positive cases were reported, however, globally, the tally was rushing uphill having the United States at the top. (Source: *India Today* 15 March 2020). On March 24, 2020, as a preventive measure, the government of India announced nationwide lockdown for 21 days, affecting the life of 1.38 billion people. The lockdown brought life to halt, and migrant laborers and their families faced existential crisis for food and other basic amenities. The government and the people at large tried to serve food packets, medicines and other items. However, prolonged lockdown broke down the patience, resulting in mass exodus from different parts of country, where people started walking on foot to travel hundreds of miles from their workplace to their native homes. This was a testing time for the administration and police to win the confidence of people at a critical stage of life. Police winning the confidence of people reflected in series of media coverage.

I was posted as Joint Director of the Central Bureau of Investigation of India at New Delhi Headquarters (hereafter CBI). The Director CBI held a meeting with senior ranks of the Bureau to percolate below ranks the instructions regarding the pandemic received from the Indian Government. The biggest challenge for the police leadership across India was to enable confidence among work force on ground. Police being a nodal agency and the visible face of the government, handling this pandemic was a first-time experience and an uphill task. Police were putting their own lives at risk. My memory fails to remember any precedent where pandemic became such a global threat to the entire humanity. The boundaries of developed and developing or underdeveloped nations shattered. Everyone from rags to rich was sailing in the same boat, yearning for safety for life. The international and national agencies handling the pandemic were cluelessly changing the virus protocols; medical care utterly facing crisis of resources, and more so settling the prescriptions.

As a senior police officer, I witnessed various facets of life having varied shades during this unique, bewildering crisis. The pandemic has affected people in multi-pronged manners.

I—Personal Observations

Born and brought up in the rural part of district Meerut of Uttar Pradesh, India, I hardly dreamed to be a police officer since "power" never fascinated me. I was happily pursuing MPhil/PhD from Jawaharlal Nehru University (JNU), New Delhi. Probably, destiny designed for me to don the Khakhi (uniform). I cleared the Civil Service Examination in 1996 and was allotted the Indian Police Services (IPS), and fortunately landed in the State of Uttar Pradesh, my home state. I was elated, but it was a daunting challenge before me to transform and enable (mentally and physically) myself to be a responsive cop worthy of serving people. I did my best to tear off my fear and inhibitions, inculcate desired traits for a policeman for "public." After serving in police for over 25 years, I pray to God, if there is rebirth, I always want to be a cop. This service gave me the utmost opportunity and confidence to provide instant justice especially for the unheard and dejected. In my village there was no policeman, so aspirations of people from my area, relatives and friends were too high from my position.

In 2020, the First Phase of the pandemic was experimental in nature. Protocols were changing frequently, no one was sure what to do exactly. Spread of disease was the major concern, and people were afraid of touching surface. Mask became the face of people. Sanitizer and masks became new normal. Since the beginning, I was apprehensive that the virus might be in the microbial family . . . being an airborne disease that we learned about during Microbiology sessions during MPhil in JNU. Later, this fact was duly acknowledged, and inhaling steam stand in the treatment protocol.

In the First Phase, the United States was worst hit having highest toll for life. I started learning more about the disease, its prevention and cure. I was in constant touch with eminent doctors and domain experts, since I worked with many of them during my research days. In order to educate people and police, social media platforms were used on regular basis. On WhatsApp and Facebook wall, I started posting the protocols, especially Dos and Don'ts regarding pandemic. Police in India was the first responder, always intersecting the public. Several policemen of various ranks and their families were afraid and concerned for their safety and were in constant touch with me. It was my earnest duty, as I perceived, to fittingly educate people. "Education and apt awareness" are complementary and necessary to combat dire challenge in life. Fortunately, the First Phase of the virus was slightly better in India in terms of toll on life compared to the Western world. In CBI, people got infected during the first phase, but the damage was limited despite the panic remaining throughout.

After serving nearly ten years on foreign deputation in the United Nations Office on Drugs and Crime (UNODC), and with the Central Bureau of Investigation (CBI) on central government deputation, I joined back Uttar Pradesh Police, the largest force of the country, as the Chief of Anti-Terror Squad (ATS). This coveted organization has multi-pronged role for broadly combating against anti-national activities and works in tandem with the central and state agencies. I was delighted to lead ATS UP, a dream team, since it works silently and provide ample scope for innovation and use of technology. Further, I went on deputation in early 2012 when I was serving as SSP (Operations), ATS. I had a hidden dream to lead this organization, which now became a reality. With tremendous support of the government and dedicated team of officers and subordinate ranks, ATS UP started conquering new heights, initiated new units at various locations in the state including "Economic Analysis Wing" (EAW), etc.

My passion for ensuring quality investigation with long-serving experience in CBI India helped me in shaping investigation protocols to the best of my capacity. I poured entire learnings gathered from professional and academic pursuits. I always believe in "Justice," and never anxious securing for conviction rate. I stand that "Fairness in investigation is the precursor to Fair Trial." There is pressing global need for enabling scientific temper in administration of justice. If an investigator has collected quality evidence, conviction is bound to follow. Poor quality of evidence leads to miscarriage of justice both in terms of releasing the culprit and convicting an innocent. As a leader of force, it's satisfying if your organization gets appreciation from all corners, and so was the ATS UP.

But, the graph of progress is hardly linear, and here came the roadblock from the Second Phase of the virus in India. The Second Phase of the pandemic mainly hit North India between early April to mid-May 2021, and this period was truly nightmare. In the first week of April 2021, I suffered from fever with mild cough; it was the virus. I quarantined myself at home with due precautions and medical consultation, but to avoid panic, I did not disclose it at home. Panic deteriorates you faster, breaking one's physical and mental strength to combat with enemy (here the pathogen). Almost in a week, I was totally fit, and resumed duty. I believed that sustained physical fitness regime helps to strengthen lymph system and improve immunity. During this time, the graph of infected patients started rocketing, and I could visualize that this pandemic phase would be horrendous. On social media platforms and other public domains, so many advisories were floating that even educated persons were utterly confused. Hence, we had to devise a system with credence and reliability.

I had nearly 1000 individuals directly under my command but were located at nearly 20 locations across Uttar Pradesh. Including their family members, we must serve for at least 5000 persons having age ranging from neonatal babies to old-aged parents. In addition, other police officers and personnel, relatives, friends and public known to me were also looking for our services/advisory. Everywhere the medical facilities were of varied nature. We opened a new segment for the pandemic with dedicated staff in the Control Room at ATS HQ serving 24/7 under the command of an efficient and dedicated officer. A WhatsApp Group was also created. Every member of ATS was supplied the mobile numbers of officers, including mine, for communication in case of any emergency.

In the third week of April 2022, my wife and both children (pursuing graduation—BALLB) at Lucknow and my brother's family at Ghaziabad got infected on the same day. We live together with our mother and mother-in-law, with age close to 80. Luckily, both were safe, but their protection was of utmost concern. I was the only healthy person at home to serve my family in sickness. In addition, I was monitoring the threatening conditions of people around me in ATS and others. The number of people around falling infected was increasing rapidly. It was high time of crisis and people were crying to get beds in the hospitals, oxygen cylinders to breathe, medicines to cure, and equipment to monitor. I was receiving calls from people in tears to help for saving their loved ones. It was terrifying and visible threat to humanity.

Despite putting best efforts by the doctors, we lost our cousin at Meerut Hospital fighting the virus. She was a little bit older than me and we played together during our childhood. Despite her having little opportunity for formal education, I rate her brilliant and forward looking. It was a devastating moment for me and the entire family. In her cherished memories, I failed to hold my tears, numbed with sorrow. Everyday, receiving news of losing people known to us hurts deeply. Everyone has lost a near dear one during the ongoing pandemic. The only grace was that in ATS, despite large number of people suffered from mild to severe infections, everyone was safe.

II–Social Expectations and Economic Challenges

The pandemic brought plethora of expectations and challenges. It reunited human beings to cooperate and to stand together during the hour of crisis. The people and government extended hands to support people, served food stuff and medicines in order to fulfill basic needs. Public-spirited persons and organizations helped people in crisis. It affected the lifestyle of people; loneliness was biting. Mask, sanitizer, quarantine, pandemic became household names. People learned to live in crisis and learned lessons that disease does not discriminate on the turf of haves or have-nots. Immunity and heath care became the foremost concern to everyone.

Mass exodus of people from different corners of India, even on bare feet with children, women and old aged illustrates that people feel safe at their native home in time of crisis. People expect more responsive and compassionate governance at time of crisis. State must spend adequate budget to raise and upgrade facilities for medical care. Every life is precious. Pandemic is a disaster, irrespective of natural or manmade, it must be dealt with with utmost professionalism. There must be an elaborative system to handle such crisis. No politics, no business–only truth.

During the pandemic, people lost life, health and job. Post-pandemic financial challenges are ongoing and worldwide. The state must ensure social security for people in need. Several children and old-aged became orphan due to loss of earning members of their families. There are reported instances in media against officials who indulged in various corrupt practices in procurement of medicines and other items. It's time for introspection–where are we? Ethics are depleting rapidly and people are in the rut of illicit enrichment.

Despite all odds, people have shown courage, fervently participated in democratic process, and elected governments in several states including Uttar Pradesh. Life is slowly attaining normalcy. It's a silver lining for progressivism to move forward in life to ensure generational perpetuity. Together we can fight and strong human relations are the elixir of life.

III–PROFESSIONAL CHALLENGES

The pandemic crisis created several challenges in all spheres of life including professional arena. The economy cannot shut down for long. The wheel of life must move forward. During the pandemic, the concept of "Work from Home" was introduced, that enhanced digital dependence of people in all sectors. The cyber warriors brought new solutions for remote interactions. Team, Zoom and various other interactive platform brought the workforce sitting together virtually irrespective of physical distances. I remember in the Central Bureau of Investigation, the digitization was long awaited. The pandemic revolutionized work from home through the Computer Application System (CAS). Initially, using CAS was compulsory, but now, the entire office passionately works efficiently on paperless system promoting environment protection with ease of file movement and tracking. CAS became new normal in CBI despite now working from office. Similar practices were broadly observed in other offices across India.

In the education sector and training institutes, the pandemic restrictions facilitated distant learning. The digital platforms have created online classroom environment imparting knowledge to the students and professionals. Distance has been shortened and experts need not to fly or travel for delivering talks—now it's a Global Classroom.

IV—Takeaway

Every crisis is a voyage of learning and an assessment for improvement; and the pandemic is no exception. It taught us handling and living with prolonged life-threatening crisis. Responsive governance is needed to handle such exigencies with professional vigor and caring aptitude. On social front, compassion, unity, reciprocity and gratitude are the attributes to withstand during difficult phase of life. "Together we can fight" must be the tagline for our society. Those who exploit people in crisis are the worst enemy of humanity and such black sheep must be identified, exposed and ostracized. On economic front, adequate budget must be apportioned for better health and quality education. People must elect responsive government without getting trapped into disruptive and ulterior considerations like caste, creed, regionalism, religion or money. Professionally, research and development activities must be promoted with adequate funds and recognition. The pandemic forced us to realize that pandemics are beyond geopolitical boundaries, not discriminating between rich or poor. The virus is going to stay with us like other pathogens; so, we must learn the art of living in crisis. **Humanity is one—we can survive if we unite—not divide.**

Dr. G.K. Goswami, IPS

Dr. G.K. Goswami, MSc, LLM, PhD (Medicinal Chemistry), PhD (Law), DSc (Forensic Sciences and Law) hails from Allipur Alampur village in the district Meerut, Uttar Pradesh, India. His father was a farmer and school-teacher and mother a homemaker. He joined IPS in 1997 in the State of Uttar Pradesh.

Currently, he is pursuing the **Fulbright-Nehru Academic and Professional Fellowship (2020-21)** as Flex Awardee at the Cornell Law School, Ithaca, New York, to study on Wrongful Convictions and Innocence Project. Until March 2022, he served as the Chief of Anti-Terror Squad (ATS) of the State of Uttar Pradesh (UP), in the rank of Additional Director General of Police. Earlier, on deputation to the Government of India, he served as Joint Director, Central Bureau of Investigation (CBI), India. As an expert on organized crime, he rendered his service to the United Nations Office on Drug and Crime (UNODC) and extensively travelled across globe to share experience on wide spectrum of issues related to policing. In the State of UP, he served as District Police Chief (SSP) in various districts including Lucknow, Agra, Varanasi, NOIDA, Moradabad, Etawah, etc.

Hon'ble President of India has honored him **2nd Bar by decorating three times with Police Medal for Gallantry, the highest national award for Police,** and the Police Medal for Meritorious Service conferred by the Hon'ble President of India. His Excellency the Governor of Uttar Pradesh has also conferred upon him Gold Medal for Gallantry.

He did MSC (Chemistry) and LLM and also studied Life Science in Jawaharlal Nehru University Delhi. He earned double PhD in Medicinal Chemistry, and Law. He won several Gold Medals and Commendations in his legal academic endeavor of LL.B. and LL.M. The National Forensic Sciences University (NFSU), Gandhinagar has recently awarded him D.Sc. (Post-doctoral degree); and he became FIRST INDIAN to have this prestigious academic distinction. He is Honorary Professor of Law and Forensic Sciences in four top universities in India. Dr. Goswami is an avid writer especially on exploring interface of law and sciences and has authored several articles in various journals of international repute. He has authored four books in the field of DNA forensics and assisted reproduction.

Mobile: +91 8800111999
Email: **goswamigk.ips@gmail.com**

MAKING IT THROUGH THE PANDEMIC: HOW TO OVERCOME WORRY, FEAR AND SELF-DOUBT
BY ANDREA WOOLF

It hit me hard getting diagnosed with triple negative breast cancer, one of the most aggressive forms of cancer–and in the middle of the pandemic no less!

This was a really BIG deal! Up until then I have been blessed to have had relatively few health challenges in my entire life. With all the experience I have as a zesty business and personal coach for over twenty-five years and knowing better, even I have been overwhelmed at times about everything that's going on in my medical journey, such as navigating all the doctors, taking all the tests and, "star of the show," starting chemo with the strongest cocktail on the market. It has been truly OMG! However, once I got over the initial shock, I made a commitment at the very beginning of this adventure to wear sparkly bling every day to remind myself to focus on the brighter side of life. Then I quickly concluded that I couldn't imagine myself just sitting around worrying and doing nothing. I am all about making a difference in the world, especially with wonderful women just like you. And I coach letting go of worry with everyone who comes into my world.

Here's what I know: At any given time, most of us women are dealing with something significant in our life that's truly challenging. And the main reason for that is because we all wear so many hats. For example, it could be that not only are you an amazing Mom, you are also dealing with taking care of your aging parents.

Or you may be juggling organizing your work life around taking care of your kids. This is no small feat, my friend.

THE PROBLEM WITH WORRY

When you're dealing with a big challenge, it's all too easy to default to worry. And when you do, you automatically step out of being in this moment and go negative, expecting the worst. On top of this, you try to be strong for everyone around you by keeping how you're feeling to yourself. So, unless they are psychic, they have no idea what you are going through.

Does this sound like you?

BEWARE OF WORRY, FEAR AND SELF-DOUBT

It's understandable if whatever you're going through is overwhelming. In my case, all this medical stuff was a whole new world, as well as a whole new language that I didn't speak. However, I knew giving in to worry, fear and self-doubt doesn't help or solve anything. In fact, it usually makes it much worse!

And going it alone makes everything much tougher than it needs to be. So, I refused to give in to worry.

WORRY IS EXPECTING THE WORST IN THE FUTURE

When you find yourself giving in to worry, it means that you're letting those gremlins–those negative voices in your head—run the show. And this will definitely **not** make anything easier. In fact, it will only make everything harder. I'm here to remind you that it doesn't have to be this way. Worry is all about expecting the worst out in the future. In truth, you only have

STEP INTO YOUR POWER AND TRANSFORM

this moment right now and then this moment right now. In other words, a series of "now moments."

CLIENT STORY #1: HOW WORRY IMPACTED SARAH

Sarah has her own business and a busy personal life. She is married with children and takes care of her aging parents—all in all, a whirlwind of a life.

What she didn't realize was that she was worrying herself to distraction and she wasn't consciously aware of it. She felt like she was constantly juggling. All she knew was that she was getting more and more frustrated. She would worry about how the next day, the next week, the next month was going to go in her business. She would also worry about not being a good mom or wife and struggled to find a way to spend more time with her children and her husband. And then, when she was home, she would worry about what was happening in her business. So, she was never being fully present in her life.

What she didn't realize was that all her worrying was impacting every-one around her. So the very thing that Sarah didn't want—for example, friction with her husband—was exactly what she was causing and creating. You're probably familiar with the phrase "Be careful what you wish for, you might just create it." That was what was happening—the worst. Even her children were staying away from her as much as they could. And then, to add insult to injury, Sarah started to "'what if" herself—in other words, asking herself unanswerable, negative questions. For example, "What if my business fails?" None of the questions that she was asking herself led anywhere positive or inspiring. And she had no idea that what she was doing was giving herself permission to stay unconsciously conscious. When we started working together, Sarah very quickly saw that she was playing the victim inside her own life. Then she embraced the idea that she could choose how her life could be.

One of my most important assertions is: **You always have choice, especially when you don't think you do. And where you always have choice is how you choose to react to what shows up in your life.** Sarah grasped this very quickly. She started choosing consciously. When I asked her how she would ideally like her business to be going, she had a wonderful list of ideas. We started working on the list and amazing results started showing up very quickly. Then we focused on her relationship with her husband. As soon as she started choosing powerfully, she shifted, and it transformed to being loving and harmonious. Then she naturally reconnected lovingly with her kids—and now her life was a dream come true.

THERE IS NO RULE YOU HAVE TO WORRY

Nowhere is it written that you must default to worry. Being in the NOW and choosing powerfully will help you breathe, which in turn will give you access to remembering who you really are and how truly powerful you are. Always remember, suffering is optional. You do not have to go it alone. Choosing to do so will only make it harder.

CLIENT STORY #2: HOW FEAR AFFECTED CHARLOTTE

Charlotte was being driven by her fears and she had no idea whatsoever that they were insidiously running the show.

Her biggest fear was of being rejected. How often are you worried about that? For example, when you're networking for your business, or asking for a promotion at work and you don't even open up that conversation for fear of rejection? *You have to be smart to make it this complicated!* This is exactly what Charlotte was doing. She was overcomplicating. Her business had reached a plateau and she was totally frustrated.

STEP INTO YOUR POWER AND TRANSFORM

The next fear that Charlotte was experiencing is very common. It's like a double-sided coin. One side is fear of failure, and the other is fear of success. There were times when she didn't even realize she was holding back because she didn't want to be more successful than her husband. She feared the impact that would have on their marriage. And the other side of the coin was fear of failure. Have you ever thought about playing a bigger game in business or in life and then you became overly consumed with the unanswerable question, "What if it doesn't work out"? Or alternatively you create a big vision and goals and then get gripped by fear, asking yourself, "What if I don't achieve everything?" The number one reason most people do not create their vision and set goals is the fear of failure. Charlotte was in a veritable swirl around which direction to take her business, fearing alternately playing a bigger game and becoming more successful, or sinking into the morass of failure. She was in a complete holding pattern.

Have you ever felt this kind of paralysis that fear can create? This was perfectionism in action. It can be mind-numbingly paralyzing when you won't take the first step towards your dream because you don't know how to do it all perfectly. Charlotte was my superstar perfectionist client. Our challenge was to help her overcome this. One aspect of her perfectionism was the fear of looking silly or stupid. This is very predominant, especially for women in our "civilized" Western world, because we are trained from a very young age that image is everything.

Charlotte had this inner fear and she had no idea to what degree it was causing her to hold back. I am happy to share that Charlotte started to take her power back and overcome each fear. As we brought each fear to the surface, she saw which side of the coin she had been choosing all this time and flipped it, because it was no longer serving her. She wanted to live a happy, fear-free life. And, as she relaxed, so did everything and everyone around her. Her business and life quickly shifted in a positive direction.

Think about how you can take some of these ideas into your life and let go of fears that you weren't even aware of.

CLIENT STORY #3: HOW SELF-DOUBT IMPACTED GLORIA

Gloria was feeling tired all the time and she realized that she wanted to change that. Has that ever happened to you? In Gloria's case, this tide of exhaustion came from second-guessing herself. She would often doubt herself by questioning everything she was doing. She was basically driving herself crazy. When you do this, you feel like you're standing on quicksand. And the way that you're being with yourself makes the ground feel softer and softer.

In addition, she was listening to everyone's opinions. When you do that, everyone is eager to share their opinions. In fact, they'll offer them even when unasked because you've trained them to do that.

Gloria was miserable. She was suffering her way through day after day, all caused by her self-doubt. She was focusing on the negative, and she would come up with every excuse under the sun. She was coming from this place of "I can't because," "that won't work because"—all negative, and she was driving everyone around her crazy. As the leader of the pack in her business, this did not work too well as a strategy. Have you ever experienced that? Where the leader was full of self-doubt and negative? Where the leader was very weak, and the team was running the show? That's how it was going, caused by Gloria's self-doubt and self-questioning.

In her personal life, her children could not get clear answers from her. And they could not count on her because she would keep changing her mind. It was absolutely chaos. And her husband was worn out because they could never do anything due to Gloria being so negative. So, their life was on hold and nothing was working right.

Just like worry and fear, overcoming self-doubt is very simple. The first step is to replace the negative with the positive—because if you allow the negative to sustain, it will. One of the first things that we worked on with Gloria was for her to embrace that she was good enough just the way she was. She had a tape running in her head repeating, "I'm not good enough." The simple way to eliminate it was to replace it with the opposite, "I am good enough." Or, even better, 'I'm amazing!'" This changed everything. She started to have a spring in her step, and she was much easier to be around.

Remember to embrace your magnificence! Be bold and bodacious and be excited to be you because there is only **ONE YOU.** When you do this, your energy will go up and you'll have amazing vitality. And who knows, you may even enjoy your life.

5 Keys to Overcome Worry, Fear and Self-Doubt

- Be in this moment right now — vs. worrying about the future
- Expect the best — vs. the worst
- Where you choose to focus determines your experience of life—choose to focus on the positive
- Embrace Your Magnificence! — Believe in yourself
- K.I.S.S. — Keep It Simple Superstar vs. Overcomplicating

Shift Your Focus

Now that you have heard all about overcoming worry, fear, and self-doubt, let me help you manage all three by taking you by the hand to give you an even more powerful place to focus. Back when I started my cancer journey, I meditated on how I could make a difference with wonderful women just like you. And the inspiration that came to me is my **"Count Your Blessings—Shift Your Focus to Transform Your Life" Program.**

How I Can Help You

Over the last 25+ years, as a zesty business and personal coach, I have helped hundreds of women in all walks of life overcome whatever was holding them back and then create and live the life that they love. As a result, they went from settling to sizzling! And it all started for each one of them with shifting their focus.

Here's What Count Your Blessings Is All About

I created **"Count Your Blessings"** because I see so often how easy it is to get caught up in what's urgent and screaming the loudest, which almost always leads to focusing on the negative. By focusing on the positive, it will change everything. Over the 30 days, the quick and easy daily practice will highlight the gifts, miracles and blessings that are there for the noticing in every area of your life. In addition, you'll be a treasured member of the private **Count Your Blessings** community where you'll connect with other like-minded and like-hearted women just like you—and where everyone will be encouraged, supported and celebrated!

It's About the Gifts, Miracles and Blessings

If you are worrying, fearful or self-doubting, this is for you. Over the 30 days, the gifts, miracles and blessings will be revealed in different areas of your life. And you will discover even more about yourself.

AND IT'S MY GIFT TO YOU!

It's Time to Get Started

Come experience the transformation as you shift your focus. Get started right now and go to **AndreaWoolf.com/CYBGift.** Can't wait to welcome you into the program!

To your magnificence!—Andrea Woolf

Andrea Woolf

Andrea Woolf is the founder of Ignited Women of Impact, a vibrant community of women entrepreneurs and executives ready to change the world. She is also a speaker, international bestselling co-author, and coach extraordinaire who inspires women to stand out, speak up and shine in their business or career and entire life.

andrea@andreawoolf.com
http://andreawoolf.com
http://andreawoolf.com/facebook
http://andreawoolf.com/linkedin

Section 3:
OWN YOUR GREATNESS
NO MATTER WHAT

SOLITUDE, SERVICE AND SELF-CARE
BY AMEALYA BLAKE

I was living inside my grief.

The weekend the world shifted in 2020 was the weekend my family was shifting back into togetherness after our world shifted eleven years before. Our father, the light and leader of our family was kidnapped and presumed murdered. The eleven years that followed was like the 2020 pandemic. Our family landscape was forever altered and those that remained dealt with their grief in their own way.

I was living inside my grief.

In March 2020, my sister and I flew to Atlanta to be with our brother, the first time any of my siblings and I got together to honor our dad's passing. On March 16, the actual anniversary of when our dad went missing, I was notified that my hometown of Oakland, California, had a shelter-in-place order that went into effect that day. It was like a history flashback. There I was March 16, 2009, out shopping as it was my boyfriend at the time's birthday, when I got the news about my dad. There I was March 16, 2020, celebrating my dad's memory, when I got the news about our shelter-in-place order. Landscape shifts in moments of joy.

What did this newest shift have to teach me? It boiled down to, I had been living inside of my grief. Living inside of my grief in a way that had me playing small. In a way that had me existing and surviving, yet not truly *thriving*. Sure, I had accomplishments. I was conditioned to excel and regardless of what I was going through, that built-in servo mechanism always kicks in. Yet it wasn't at the level of fully experiencing the *feeling* of the accomplishments. The pandemic created a great pause and what it brought up was the *feelings*, the feelings I had suppressed in my grief. The *feelings* that were coming to the surface as the world experience the collective grief of a change in social norms and our way of life.

Solitude, service and self-care were the medicine that I used to address the feelings that were coming to the surface.

Six feet social distance orders, shelter-in-place rules and suddenly everyone was in a time-out. I had started the practice of meditation after the loss of my dad and suddenly, I had plenty of enforced time to meditate. **Spending time in solitude gives you plenty of opportunity to look at yourself, if you're willing.** Suddenly there's no distraction of going out, hanging with friends, a million and one activities that all of a sudden were on pause. **As I continued to look at myself, I saw the self I was being and the self I desired to be. There was a chasm between the two and I tried to do what all my spiritual books, teachers and guides say: practice forgiveness.**

Forgiveness of all my perceived faults, shortcomings and mistakes. Forgiveness for not getting to know me a long time ago and to know what the real me truly wants. Forgiveness for not seeing that I didn't allow myself to grieve the biggest loss I had endured to date and how that can and should shift the image I held of myself. After all, the image I held of myself had a dad to walk me down the aisle, a dad to visit the new home I purchased. That image is no more. Forgiveness work, is work. Yet work I committed myself to. I started using the phrase: "Feel it to heal it," taken from the book *The Presence Process.* As I started to feel an emotion, I allowed myself to question: what do I need to forgive here?

During the pandemic, forgiveness work was a focus of several groups I belonged to. My spiritual community, Heart and Soul Center of Light, offered several classes, not to mention world-class Sunday Service messages on the importance and power of forgiveness work. The virtual community Wake

Up Everybody, a spiritual community that formed during the pandemic and became a lifeline for so many during shelter-in-place, was another source of forgiveness work. Each session, a facilitator would present a topic on life and somehow, it often boils down to forgiveness of self and others.

Service. My life has been big on service. I've been a nurse since I was born. I say that as the oldest of seven; nursing just becomes a way of life. I officially became a nurse at nineteen years old, while I was at Utica College. Now at 41, serving as a nurse has been a rewarding journey with too many patient moments to count. **During the pandemic, service took on a new experience. My concept of service expanded now to: how do I serve my community in a greater way? I guess it was a question I was seeking internally as opportunities started to present themselves.**

In December 2019, I was studying to become a certified meditation coach. I was initiated into meditation after the loss of my dad. Over time, after experiencing the personal benefits, I realized it was now a lifelong endeavor. That holiday season in December, I decided to share a medi-tation I was studying with some colleagues on the floor where I worked at Kaiser Permanente. After we came out of the session, my good friend Arlene said, "We should start a meditation group!" I said sure! **The first Monday in January 2020, we started our meditation group. Along came the pandemic, and our Meditation Monday group went virtual.** Suddenly more people joined. Eventually another good friend, Roxanne, recom-mended I join the the MindFul Hub at Kaiser Permanente. The MindFul Hub is a collection of Mindfulness practitioners who volunteer to share their mindfulness practices with the Kaiser community. I met with the MindFul Hub and eventually moved my Meditation Monday to their platform. Now Meditation Monday serves Kaiser's eight regions. **As the pandemic contin-ued, more and more people started to see the benefit of having a mindful practice as a resilience tool—myself being a number one champion.**

2020 was the year I served as the President of Oakland Uptown Toastmaster's Club. Toastmasters is an international public speaking club and has been instrumental in my growth of self-expression. That year, I implemented mindful moments to our weekly club agenda as an opportunity to pause and get grounded as we start our meeting. It's a practice that continued after I moved on from the Presidency role and a legacy I am grateful to be part of. Being of service to these communities was a balm as I continued to move through the pandemic.

Self-care. **Self-care has become a buzz word.** Everyone is getting on the self-care train. And I am happy. **Yet self-care is more than just bubble baths, massages and foot spas. Self-care is how you care for the inner self, the inner you that needs nourishment as much as the physical body.** First, you have to get in touch with that inner you. That's where solitude comes in. Then you have to be honest with what the needs are of the inner you. Do you need connection, passion, purpose, appreciation, love, therapy . . . etc.? Only you know what the real you needs. Then start by giving yourself what you need. I realized I needed therapy. So I joined groups: spiritual study groups, I got a prayer partner, I took virtual workshops. More than that, I formed study groups, created and delivered workshops. I came to understand that the best form of therapy is self-expression—expressing your authentic truth. I still have a ways to go. So I keep on with my spiritual study groups, prayer partners and creating workshops. These are my sources of self-care practices and caring for my inner me.

When I think about the bright spots of the pandemic, the lesson that stands out for me is that I can live inside of grief and still find the path to thrive. That grief is often the catalyst for moving all the busi-ness of life out of the way, so we can get to the business of a thriving self. The pandemic has been an opportunity to pause in solitude, look at how and where I am serving and how am I factoring self-care in the mix. **The pandemic still lingers. How are you using this time of self-reflection? In what areas are you serving? What are some of your self-care tools? You can live inside grieving what was, and still *thrive* with what is!**

Bio:

Amealya Blake

Amealya Blake teaches mindfulness tools to teams and organizations so they can handle day-to-day stress with ease and grace. A registered nurse and certified meditation coach by training, she has worked as a public health educator in New York, Los Angeles and the Greater Bay Area. She speaks on the topic of holistic health and has been a guest on NPR, NY1, NBC and ABC. In her spare time, she enjoys hiking, meditation and exploring the hidden gems of Northern California.

Facebook: Amealya Blake
Instagram: Amealya_Blake

CLIMATE CRISIS: PURPOSE-TO-POSSIBILITIES
BY UPENDRA GIRI

The pandemic could have been a uniting experience for humanity. As I start reflecting on the recent past of the most stressful time of our life, there was a silver lining. I am finding myself in between the closing rush of these yet again very intense weeks and a deep sense of need to look back towards the last two years and reflect on "how it started—how it's going." While I am happy and grateful for so many things, I cannot help but wonder, what are the lessons for the future? For me, the most important question today is what is my purpose of being? I started looking at a few established practices such as Ikigai, which is a Japanese concept referring to something that gives a person a sense of purpose, a reason for living. I got my hands on some very powerful tools such as The Golden Circle, an innovative concept presented by Simon Sinek in his very popular TED Talk and book *Start With Why*. According to him, using this model can "explain how legendary leaders like Steve Jobs, Martin Luther King Jr., and the Wright brothers were able to inspire, rather than manipulate, in order to motivate people. It is the framework for the WHY."

MY WHY

I started my soul-searching and traveled down memory lane, when I entered United States of America with a dream of studying Environmental Engineering at Lehigh University. At Lehigh, I had the privilege of having Dr. Sibel Pamucku as my advisor on an environmental remediation project. I worked as a research assistant at Fritz Engineering Laboratory of Lehigh University on "utilizing scrap tires and iron slag in highway pavements."

The materials investigated under this study were scrap tires in the form of Crumb Rubber Modifier (CRM) and iron process residue aggregate referred to as Iron-Rich Material (IRM). At that time, it was a research project which paid for my tuition and stipend for my graduate degree. As I reflect today, I'm proud to share that my research work is helpful in many applications, including highways, parks, running tracks, playgrounds, etc. I see that I was already living my purpose of being on the planet and the impact I could make.

Later on, I joined NASA for its environmental remediation program and I started to develop expertise in managing large complex programs. In the meantime, I stumbled upon Project, Program and Portfolio Framework which enabled me to help individuals, teams and enterprises deliver sustainable value by bringing innovation better, cheaper and faster. It further reinforced my belief that there is symbiotic relationship between sustainable business and technology & innovation strategy: one delivers the other and, if aligned correctly, with just one pocket of spending. Once aligned, the ability to define a direction and measure progress against commonly recognized Key Performance Indicators (KPIs) which deliver environmental, social and governance (ESG) advances as well as financial performance—at pace—is key for this decisive decade as we address climate adaptation.

As I started exploring more about the work of global leaders in the recent past history of the world, it started becoming very evident that it's not climate change, it's climate crisis and the time bomb is ticking.

Let's see what some of the change makers have to say about current context and the challenge the world is facing today.

"The world must come together to confront climate change. There is little scientific dispute that if we do nothing, we will face more drought, famine and mass displacement that will fuel more conflict for decades." — Barack Obama

"The game will be won or lost in the developing countries. The United States has about half of the entire globe's innovation power. We owe it to the world to use that power to reduce green premiums and enable countries like India to say yes to these solutions." —Bill Gates, co-chair of the Bill & Melinda Gates Foundation

"Thinking ahead with a multidecade time frame allows you to take moonshots, to be very ambitious . . . Looking to 2030, we aim to run everything carbon free, 24/7. That means every query on Google, every Gmail you send, every transaction on the Google cloud will be done without emissions. We don't fully know how to get there. We need more innovation. We also need more project financing." —Sundar Pichai, chief executive officer, Alphabet Inc.

Combating the climate crisis requires an all-hands-on-deck approach, including innovation in the public–private sector to substantially reduce our nation's carbon footprint. I applaud the countries and organizations participating in the Better Climate Challenge to shrink harmful carbon emissions by 50 percent over the next decade.

For me, this is the brighter side of the pandemic. Climate change is a mammoth task, the question is what we all can do within our own capability to contribute to dealing with this daunting task.

Each situation must be tackled individually and on its own terms and the underlying cause is not always apparent. Compared to the pandemic virus, understanding climate change as a single collective threat to humanity is much more difficult. The challenge is certainly global—but the experience is often local.

RISE TO THE OCCASION–THE TIME IS NOW

Through interactions and interventions with people like Elon Musk, Dr. APJ Abdul Kalam, Bill Gates, John Doerr, Larry Page, and Ratan Tata, I discovered all of them are the most passionate leaders who built passionate organizations. They expressed their commitment and enthusiasm authentically, which is what inspires others. They inspired and challenged me too, to think big, with my purpose in my mind, passion in my heart and actions I take. I am now committed to helping more global companies develop innovative, sustainable business strategies. I have been leveraging the power of Objective and Key Results (OKRs) since early 2010 when I embarked upon an opportunity to bring India's first Education Storefront, called Samsung Smart Learning. This initiative became the foundation for the biggest edtech revolution in India.

To me, mitigating global warming inherently transcends the scope of global action. It will be achieved through concerted efforts at the global level, or it will fail. In the recent past, Earth's atmosphere reacted in surprising ways to the lowering of emissions during the pandemic, showing how closely climate warming and air pollution are linked. In the case of climate change, the nature of the threat is less immediately tangible. Therefore, raising awareness about and promoting the urgent need to address climate change becomes a political task—and the key to effective action. In recent years, substantial progress has been made; massive international mobilization, particularly of young people, has shifted politics in an eco-friendlier direction in many parts of the world. But large swaths of the public remain skeptical. Natural catastrophes—such as the historic floods, storms, and fires in Russia—create a temporary surge in attention and concern, but interest levels tend to wane rather quickly. Other crises, such as the pandemic or economic setbacks like the current rise of energy prices, tend to hold the attention of the public and of the political leaders for much longer.

MY HOW—WHAT GETS MEASURED GETS DONE

Climate diplomacy has to define common objectives, establish monitoring and review mechanisms and put in place structures for financial burden sharing. Regular climate summits serve to update the commitments and coordinate international cooperation. However, in the absence of an effective enforcement mechanism, reaching the commonly defined goals of the Paris Agreement still depends on the action of individual states. Consequently, progress is hampered by the inherent difficulties of collective action, including deficient leadership, free-riding and cumbersome decision-making. Vested interests, a partly skeptical public and an overly cautious political class are preventing vital measures from being implemented as urgently as required.

Achieving a carbon-neutral world doesn't depend on one country or even one continent. I believe everyone must contribute towards this giant which must run parallel with efforts to build effective global action through partnerships with other countries. This endeavor needs to go far beyond traditional multilateral diplomacy. All instruments—including trade, finance, development cooperation, and technology transfer—must be employed to establish the strongest possible commitment to stop or slow global warming.

Amid global financial and climate challenges, scientific collaboration and progress have been bright spots. Effective public–private partnerships and intensive international cooperation produced vaccines in record time. Through the Intergovernmental Panel on Climate Change, scientists have established a comprehensive assessment of the threat that climate change poses and identified the parameters for avoiding the most catastrophic outcomes. In both instances, cooperation among scientists has been largely uncontaminated by geopolitical and economic rivalries. Science and technology will also play a crucial role in achieving a carbon transition. However, technological innovation will not happen by itself. It will require political decisions that create economic incentives, ensuring that the necessary level of funding and direct investment reaches the most promising projects. This presupposes an unprecedented level of international cooperation among governmental and business actors.

As we emerge from the pandemic, many businesses are revisiting what success looks like for them. This is against the backdrop of global megatrends—such as the climate emergency, rising inequality, the loss of nature and the fourth industrial revolution—that are reshaping society and the operating context for business in profound ways.

The world we were born in and the world we live in today are very different. The new world is increasingly obsessed with two things: electronic gadgets and our changing climate. Our choice is clear: we need to reimagine the way in which we engage with the technology we create. Technology is in our heads, not in our hands. If we don't like what our technologies are doing to the world and to ourselves, then we all have both the power and the responsibility to make better choices today than we did yesterday. Technology and Sustainability redefines our relationship with technology and offers ways in which we can use these tools to make the world a better place through enlightened and positive engagements.

Sustainability is now a business imperative. But how do you effectively evolve from knowing to doing, empowering you to capitalize on new opportunities? A transition to a more sustainable way of doing business can only be attained by combining technology with profound system innovations and lifestyle changes.

Here is small list of things each one of us must incorporate in our daily life which would definitely make a difference. While individuals alone may not be able to make drastic emissions cuts that limit climate change to acceptable levels, personal action is essential to raise the importance of issues to policymakers and businesses.

Using your voice as a consumer, a customer, a member of the electorate and an active citizen will lead to changes on a much grander scale.

"Use your voice, use your vote, use your choice."
—Al Gore

1. Speak Up: break the silence

Get involved in your city community affairs; tell your council member, local councilors and city mayors that you think action on climate change is important. A prosperous future for the planet depends on their decisions about the environment, green spaces, roads, cycling infrastructure, waste and recycling, air quality and energy-efficient homes. Ultimately, steps to reduce carbon emissions will have a positive impact on other local issues, like improving air quality and public health, creating jobs and reducing inequality.

2. Eliminate waste: mindful consumption

The goal is to improve health and happiness while reducing carbon footprint where people drive less, walk and bicycle more, reduce household energy use and overconsumption and eat less meat and more plant-based foods. Everything we use as consumers has a carbon footprint. Avoid single-use items and fast fashion and try not to buy more than you need. Shop around for secondhand or quality items that last a long time.

3. Food habits: mindful eating

Mindful eating brings our awareness to the resources used to produce the food we consume, which we can use to lessen our intake of products that negatively impact the environment. Every time you purchase or consume food or drink, you are making a choice that will help or harm the planet and all the beings that live upon it.

4. **Everything matters: a choice will change the future**

What can individuals do? Major changes need to come from govern-ments and businesses, but scientists say some small changes in our lives can limit our impact on the climate:

- Take fewer flights
- Live car-free or use an electric car
- Buy energy-efficient products, such as washing machines, when they need replacing
- Switch from a gas heating system to an electric heat pump
- Insulate your home

For a lot of people, that can come with a sense of despair: What can one person possibly do to save a world? But there are meaningful ways indi-viduals can put pressure on corporations and policymakers to make rapid actions. Seeing our goals and progress can make difference in our lives.

The main contributors to climate change are the large corporate actors. Much of the CO2 emissions come from business-driven economic activi-ties. Business activities can also contribute to innovation and solutions to prevent and adapt to climate change.

There are various tools to help individuals, organizations, and countries, such as Project Portfolio Management, OKRs, Value Stream Management, Lean Construction, Energy Efficiency Models, Building Information Modelling (BIM). These can be used to deliver better, safer and sustainable world to move away from linear economy to circular economy.

Together we can each take steps to improve our local and global climate.

Upendra Giri

Upendra Giri is a world-renowned Project, Program and Portfolio Management leader, coach, trainer, consultant and a high-impact keynote speaker recognized globally with over 30 years of experience in providing exceptional business management services across industry sectors. Upendra firmly believes that there is a symbiotic relationship between sustainable business and technology & innovation strategy. Once aligned, they have the ability to define a direction and measure progress against commonly recognized KPIs which deliver environmental, social and governance advances as well as financial performance. He brings extensive cross-industry expertise in complex organizational change and redesign; ESG initiatives, Sustainable Infrastructure enabled through digital and green tech innovation, with a particular focus on value chain stewardship.

A true leader and evangelist of the profession, he is also the Founder and Trustee of PMI® North India Chapter and is Charter Member of TiE (The Indus Entrepreneurs). Upendra "Received the prestigious Eric Jennet Award by PMI® for his Outstanding Contributions to Global Portfolio, Program and Project Management Profession in 2009 made him first Indian and youngest professional to be bestowed with this honor." More **https://bit.ly/2RottCU**

Upendra earned his MS in civil (environmental) engineering from Lehigh University, Pennsylvania, USA, in 1994 and BSc in civil engineering in 1991 from Jamia Millia Islamia University, New Delhi, India. Born in 1969 in a village in northern India, Upendra now resides in Silicon Valley, US, and is one of the most sought-after consultants by CEOs of big multinational companies and an inspiration for budding entrepreneurs.

Email: **upendra.giri@UpBuildGlobal.com**
https://www.upbuildglobal.com
https://www.upendragiri.com
https://www.linkedin.com/in/upendragiri/
https://www.facebook.com/upendra.giri.752

THE PORTFOLIO OF POWER
BY DJ EHLERT

"Why can't I just wave a wand and make this crap all go away?"

I watched the news like everyone else.

"Let's flatten the curve."

"Fourteen days might just do it!"

"Is this the new normal? What the heck is herd immunity anyway?"

What was I going to do for fourteen whole days? I hate sitting around and wasting time. Now I was faced with two weeks of downtime? I have never been one to watch television. And the news was depressing in the extreme anyway.

I felt I had no control over all that. It's a pandemic, after all. Nothing much I can do about it, except my part in staying home to flatten that curve.

I sat. I twiddled my thumbs. That probably lasted a whole 15 minutes before I was antsy.

Then I thought, *there are all of those "someday" projects I've been putting off . . .*

THE SOMEDAY MINDSET

"What's the Someday Mindset?" you ask.

Have you ever said or thought to yourself: *Someday I'll get my life organized. Someday I'll tackle that big project. Someday I'll travel and see the beautiful landscapes or wonders of the world. Someday I'll pursue my passion for music, art, or helping other people. One of these days, someday, I'll focus on my health. Someday I'll really start meditating and working on becoming the best version of myself.*

Has that someday ever come?

Sadly for many people, "someday" never materializes.

Not because those dreams are impossible, but because they seem too big to achieve. They seem out of reach, because they haven't taken the time to break them down into small steps of focused action necessary to achieve them.

There is no perfect time to start.

When I have "x," I'll get around to starting.

When I know how to do it, I'll get on it.

When I have enough money, I'll be able to buy that gadget. Then I'll be ready to start.

When I have more time, I'll start exercising and eating better.

Waiting until you have the perfect time, gadget, bank account balance, or the perfect plan in order to begin working on your passion is the number one killer of dreams.

Why do we think we need to know and have everything to begin?

Fear is why. The fear of failure is a big one. We fear that if we risk failure and actually do fail, someone else might come along and succeed at our original idea. And that paralyzes us. What do we do then? Most of the time, we just put it off. *Someday, the timing will be perfect.* That's the Someday Mindset.

"Well, DJ, how do you know so much about all of this Someday stuff?"

I know because I've been just as guilty of it as anyone else!

We've all experienced that someday anguish and the painful realization, usually after we think it's too late to do anything about it, that someday has passed us by.

Success becomes much more predictable once we begin considering what we are doing now, alternative pathways we could take and then making our new reality through consistent actions and behaviors.

THE BRIGHTER SIDE OF THE PANDEMIC: OPPORTUNITY, NOT PROBLEM

Obviously, living through a pandemic was not part of my someday plans. It wasn't part of anyone's plan.

Life has a unique way of throwing twists and turns, setbacks, losses and downright terrible experiences of all shapes and sizes at us. We can let them beat us about and internalize them, or we can choose how to respond to the lemons of life and make some lemonade.

I chose to do what I *could* do, instead of worrying about what I could not control. I chose to make lemonade.

137

A Cluttered Garage and Cluttered Mind

"Fourteen days to flatten the curve."

I can handle that. Just fourteen days to help humanity. *OK, I am in.* Let's get this thing behind us. We can all do our part and it will make the process of getting back to our lives as we knew them much quicker.

Gulp. Well, I don't need to tell you it's been a long fourteen days. But at the time, I was simply focused on finding something to do for two weeks.

I was not entirely sure what to do with this unplanned *opportunity.* Surely my subconscious mind would help me find some solutions if I simply focused on what *could be done.*

What could I do? Clean up, for starters.

Filling up drawers, closets, attics, basements and garages with physical possessions and material items in excess of what we need is one manifestation of someday thinking.

Such was the nature of my garage.

It was a mess: two stories of crap piled up all over the place. For a couple years, I had thought, *one of these days, someday, I'll get in there and turn that garage into something useful.*

Well, someday had arrived and not because I had planned it. I had nothing else to do. There were no magic shows to perform. No educational programs to host. And my other businesses were also on hold or operating at a slow roll.

Thank god for the investments and passive income we had set up over the years because some of my business revenues had dwindled to almost zero. The investments, thankfully, were still bringing in some income for us.

Not Someday, Now!

I've always relied on my values and goal-setting as the fuel for success in my social and business ventures. That doesn't mean I've never failed. Heck no! I've failed many times, but managed to turn those into lessons learned. I try to fail *forward*, as fast as possible, so I can keep moving ahead.

I forge forward, taking calculated risks with skin in the game until I succeed or fail. I know in advance, with perseverance, I will overcome any obstacle. I will fight through it, or alter the path to make sure I am living the life I want. All this to avoid the dreaded, Someday.

For the second time in a five-year span I had moved into a larger home with more space and an outbuilding needed to run one of the businesses my wife and I have built and continue to operate.

Moving, as always, means making messes. This move was no different. The process of moving while still living and running businesses meant we had little time to completely unpack all the boxes we brought with us. There were a plethora of them still stored in the garage and attic.

Make a Mess to Clean a Mess

"How many people on the planet do you think clean out the garage like this?"

My wife and family were less than enthused at my process.

EVERYTHING OUT!

There is a method to my madness! I removed literally everything from my two-story garage and placed it in the driveway. Every automobile, all the lawn equipment, tools, boxes of who knows what was in them, leftover wood from previous projects, camping equipment, chairs, bicycles and much, much more.

When I was finished with step one, only the dust remained.

To any passersby, it probably looked like a hillbilly garage sale in progress. Thankfully, no one stopped by—probably due to the pandemic quarantine. My family was saved that embarrassment at least.

Sure, I could have swept out the dust and the leaves, put a few things away, and called it a day. But I had a grand vision of a clean, neat, organized, decluttered, and completely functional garage—one I'd always dreamed I'd have, someday.

I just grinned and focused on the mission. It's not like I was skirting other responsibilities to *over*-clean the garage. I guess I could've split up the process and gotten the same results, but it was so satisfying to stay focused on the task and achieve a superior result.

Keeping the Momentum

Once I'd swept out the dust and debris, I turned to my electric pressure washer. I spent an entire day washing the all-wood ceilings, walls, floors and the concrete slab. Then I set up some fans to begin the drying process.

The next day I went through the mess in the driveway. Three piles emerged: the stuff to keep, stuff to donate to Goodwill, and my favorite pile, the miscellaneous items and debris I would never have to think about, wonder if I still had, or allow to clutter up my mind in any way, ever again. That pile was headed to the dump!

Then it was repair time! I reframed the staircase to the second-floor loft to include a landing and handrails and repaired several holes in the loft floor I had inherited from the previous owner. I then repaired and replaced everything else not operating correctly.

Now the real work began.

Next I walked through the garage, planning the perfect place for everything left, you know, the stuff still in the driveway. *What kinds of shelving, hooks, and hangers do I need to organize everything in an efficient and optimal manner?* I spent the rest of that day erecting shelving units and installing hangers and hooks for the chairs, garden tools and sports equipment.

My Method: Focus on The Now, the Project at Hand

While I'm occasionally distracted, like anyone, I'm usually able to hyper-focus on a task, consistently and persistently working at it until I achieve what I've set out to do.

Only problem with that mindset is that for years, I had been so hyper-focused *in* my business and life I had forgotten to work *on* my life.

The brighter side of the pandemic, for me, was an opportunity to reassess everything. Seriously, everything: my family, my health, my values, relationships, goals, spiritual life, hobbies, and finances.

What better time to make sure that the foundation of my life was in order so I'd be ready for whatever came next?

The garage was not just clean; it was now a magnificent resource optimized for performance at the highest level. It was my someday garage!

It was so satisfying, I did not stop there. I kept my momentum. Now I also have a someday attic, basement, office, bedroom and closets! Whew!

I'll spare you the drama of all that. Suffice it to say it was an arduous undertaking, only possible because I knew I would enjoy the peace of mind that only an organized home can bring. I had total control and responsibility to create the experience of the someday home for our family.

Now my mind was free to concentrate on the rest of my someday projects.

A KIND OF MEDITATION

I like to read for about 30 to 60 minutes each day before going to sleep, usually self-help, self-improvement information. Many of the authors I've read promote the benefits of meditation.

I'd never really learned to meditate. Yeah, I know, another "someday" deal.

During the pandemic, I read up on meditation. I also watched YouTube videos and listened to podcasts on the topic. They were all helpful.

Something occurred to me while writing about my garage cleaning adventure. The focus on one task at a time to achieve a larger goal was, in fact, a form of meditation itself!

No, it wasn't sitting in the lotus position (something that's not necessary anyway), nor did it involve any special breathing techniques. But the process itself, clearing the clutter of my garage, was in fact, clearing the clutter of my mind. The closer I got to the former, the nearer I got to the latter.

How's that for a revelation?!

Meditation is really just focusing the mind on something small: keeping our attention on the *now* and not being drawn into the future or the past. And that's how you clean your garage, build a business, create art, or follow your dreams.

What's Next for Ol' DJ?

I am excited to be helping others to discover and achieve their Someday lives.

I have created a very simple-to-create-and-use framework to help anyone propel their dreams to become their reality.

I call it POP, the **Portfolio of Power!**

What's that all about?

It's about doing what it takes, now, not someday, to live your life as the best version of yourself.

How to carefully consider your values and how they correlate with your aspirations and dreams. How to create a personalized plan for yourself. How to assemble your goals and aspirations into a simple-to-use format and the tiny steps it will take to achieve them.

How to use both positive and negative inspiration to propel us at an accelerated rate to our dreams.

How to reward yourself along the way and be fulfilled and living with purpose.

Don't wait for Someday!

A theoretical Someday is not coming! Today is the day! Right now!

Begin the process of making your dreams a reality.

You have to make time for yourself, *right now*, to follow your passions, hobbies and interests.

If you do, you will feel more fulfilled, *now*, while working on your dreams.

The life you are living now should not be a *trial run* for your *next life*.

I have been overwhelmed with exhilaration and joy over and over after experiencing the power of realizing goals and bringing the Someday into the here and now.

Physically making a plan and consciously taking action toward it engages our powerful subconscious mind into action that will surprise us every time with ideas and solutions to propel us faster and faster to the reality we want, need and desire for ourselves and our families.

To discover more about how to harness the power of someday with your own personal Portfolio of Power, please visit **PortfolioOfPower.com**.

Someday is now.

DJ Ehlert

Dyslexia, dysgraphia, and growing up below the poverty level did not prevent DJ Ehlert from pursuing his passion for performing and promotion.

DJ Ehlert is a performance and marketing expert based in the Midwest.

DJ Ehlert is a serial entrepreneur having built several business ventures in sales, service, restaurants, consulting, retail, wholesale, agency and manufacturing.

DJ is also an author, consultant and mentor, having produced countless conventions and workshops on business development and marketing, enabling others to increase their impact and effectiveness in any business.

DJ Ehlert's clients include Landry's, Roundy's, Snap-on Tools, US Cellular, Abbott Laboratories and Intermatic Incorporated.

DJ has generated countless appearances on radio shows, newspapers, magazines and television programs generating a plethora of publicity for his clients and business ventures.

DJ Ehlert is known as The Entrepreneur Mentor and has a passion for transferring his skills to the next generation of entrepreneurs.

PEACE, RECONNECTION AND HEALING
BY JACQUELINE CLARKE

There truly is a brighter side to the pandemic. I believe how you look at crises or situations makes a big difference on how you experience it and how you prepare for it. I have found that preparing yourself mentally, physically and emotionally is extremely important.

I knew having faith would be how I would be able to get through this pandemic. In the past, I relied heavily on faith and God to get me through my own personal loss of my family members. I did this by recreating my mind, body and soul. I kept telling myself no matter how hard grief is, I am going to get through it. It was a daily reminder to me to keep moving forward, to never give up. I started with these few things to keep me motivated:

- Positive affirmations, always telling myself that "I love every part of myself"
- Eating healthy
- Exercising
- Spending time alone. I had to give myself the space to grieve

I even sought out counseling, both group and individual. The group counseling allowed me to realize that I am not alone and the individual counseling allowed me to work on my specific issues that I was dealing with my grieving. I found that being around others who were dealing with similar situations really helped with my healing process. It's all in due time when you are ready.

During this pandemic, so many people suffered sudden losses. No warning, no time to prepare. I knew that I had been prepared to help my near and dear ones to get through their loss while I was going through my own. **As I reflect back today, I am amazed to see the huge changes within myself with small simple steps that I took—one day at a time.**

I truly believe that through loss of life, we are never the same. Nor should we be. It forever changes us. We either get more compassionate or become bitter. For me, choosing to become more compassionate, especially with myself, was the best decision in helping me heal. Letting go! Praying and giving it to God. I realized that with all my loss, pain and suffering, I would never be the same, nor should I. This is how we grow.

Although it has been many years since my own family passed away, I never forgot the people that were there for me and my family during our loss. There were a few that didn't know how to be there for us during our loss and our suffering. Therefore, we lost connection with one another. Another decision I made during the pandemic was to do whatever it took to not isolate myself. Even though we were in a lockdown and physically couldn't go anywhere. I decided to reach out to lost connections. I gained a lot of confidence, wisdom, knowledge and resilience by doing this. It further helped with my healing process. It takes years and even decades to heal from a loss. This allowed me to help others. I shared with my family how I was able to get through my pain and suffering. I would reach out to my family members. I was proactive. I didn't wait for them to contact me.

Technology was the key factor that helped me stay in touch. I contacted them by FaceTime, Messenger, texting and/or calling. I would reassure them that they would get through it. To have faith in God. I would tell them I loved them. They would have good and bad days. Most importantly, reminding them that everyone has their own way of healing. Two people grieving from the same loss will react differently. And that's okay. Each one of us is unique in how we process our emotions. Don't compare yourself to others. I checked in with them regularly to make sure they were taking care of themselves and that they didn't feel alone. These are the key ingredients in their grieving that I believe will work for many of us. I suggested getting rest, eating, exercising and reaching out to their close friends and family, checking in on them. Most neighborhoods or cities have local crisis or grieving centers, so I suggested them to contact their grieving center. Most offer free counseling services, both group and individual. I took the pandemic as an opportunity to reconnect with my in-laws. They were great to me while I was married. But we lost connection with each other after my husband passed away. We had some unresolved issues that I wanted to complete.

Mending the relationships with my grandkids and great-grandkids were just as important. The pandemic made me realize I didn't want to carry any grudges. I made it a point to resolve these issues.

We just never know when it's our time. Some relationships have been resolved; others have not. But regardless of the outcome, I know I did my part by reaching out. This alone gives me peace. I want to live with no regrets.

During the pandemic, I realized focusing on myself was a form of self-care. I was able to give more to others. I worked even deeper on myself emotionally, mentally and physically, so that I could be there for them—giving my family and myself a better me.

The biggest decision I made during the pandemic was to relocate out of state to Arizona. This was an opportunity of a lifetime. I knew I so deserved this. This move would be taking my healing process even deeper. I realized during the pandemic, for me to truly heal, I must move out of state and have more time for myself. I had moved several times in the Bay Area; however, it didn't help in my full recovery. I guess it's a true statement: "We NEVER heal in places we have had pain." I had to remove myself from being codependent. I had to set boundaries, living with less daily stress. The move once again forced me to come out of my comfort zone, facing my fears head-on, traveling back and forth to see my family, hoping and praying this move would be healing for me as well as my family members.

Part of my healing process through the pandemic was that I re-visited places where I endured the most pain and suffering. I was able to see in all the places that I needed to release the hold of and let go. It was time to stop replay of the painful moments in my head.

My journey in life continues: to live the rest of my life happy, healthy and traveling the World. To fall more in love with myself and others. The true brighter side of my pandemic was that I realized I wanted to live without any regrets. For that to happen, I **had to take some major actions, put myself out of my comfort zone and love myself so that I could finally heal, to be a gift to my family by becoming a better version of myself. To re-connect with my family. To continue to allow others in my life.**

I'm dedicating this chapter to all my grandkids and great-grandkids,
Shyanne, William. Great-granddaughter Harlow Rose and brother.
Angela, great-grandkids Alaya & Dallas, William Ra'him, Gary, Willow, Jabari,
Daysia and Devin, Diavonne & Dante.
Michante, Erianna, Michele, DaMillion & DeMarco
Charles and his kids,
Chosen and his kids
Jovan
KeAngela, Karter
Keariah, Keziah
Kham Vanity
Kaliyah
Paris and Great Granddaughter Ne'Ana
Shanitta and Great Grandson Kingston
Steven and his kids
Julian
Chase

My heart is overwhelmed with joy when my grandkids call me Nana, grandma, great-grandma and granny "Jackie."

My hope and prayers are to continue connecting with my family! Always look to the brighter side . . . have faith and have hope.

Jacqueline Clarke

Jacqueline Rose Clarke is a woman who has persevered through her own personal tribulations. She is originally from Cheyenne, Wyoming. Jacqueline loves life. She is a mother and grandmother and has raised kids for over 40 years. She is an entrepreneur with Vasayo and an independent brand partner who loves to network. Jacqueline is a healthy, enthusiastic wellness practitioner. She enjoys working out, walking, running and swimming. Her other pastimes are spent with her family and friends. Her motto is You can change you.

Facebook: Jacqueline Clarke
Instagram: live_life_wise_jclarke
Website: **LifeWise.biz/jclarke60/enrollment/step-2**
Email: **Jbaby1960@yahoo.com**

HOW I KEPT BALANCE AND HARMONY DURING THE PANDEMIC
BY MINH DANNERSTEDT, PH D

Following the course of the history of mankind, we have seen ups and downs, we have seen wars and peace, we have seen epidemics, we have seen sufferings, killings . . . Humans live and learn, experience through discoveries and mistakes, bright times and dark times.

In my life, I have experienced normal life, war times, separation, hope, as many people in different countries have.

Recently, my father, who lived alone, became older and weaker and as I am his only child living close to him, I became the caretaker, to stay close to my father and caring as much as I could.

I was feeling lucky that I could devote my time to care for my father. He took this time to create peace and calmness to himself, and I could benefit and learn deep understanding of the spiritual messages of the alignment of mind–body–spirit at any age, as long as we are alive.

Right after my father passed away, the world was facing a difficult time of the pandemic. I did not have the time to mourn the loss of my father yet and I had to switch my heart and live through this pandemic time, as everybody around the world—a difficult and uncertain time with emotional, spiritual, financial and especially psychological challenges, where there was fear, doubts, worries, uncertainties.

As in everything from any dark side at any time, there is always a brighter side somewhere if we choose to keep calmness, positivity, hope and the wisdom of living in balance and harmony with the nature surrounding us and the vast universe.

I have learnt and applied energy self-healing and healing others, since more than 30 years, I applied energy healing to support my health and mental clarity. I was very thankful that I have learned these techniques to implement every day in my life, for myself, my family and others.

I could self-heal and heal my family, friends and many people I know during this time, on energetic level, to create balance and calmness to our body–mind–spirit, on physical, emotional and spiritual. This kept me in peace and calmness. I connect, trust the Universe and the good nature.

I want to share with you here what had brought a brighter side to my life during the pandemic.

When we can connect to the High power, the Universe, the Cosmos, it is like connecting with our source, our roots. There is a connection that uplifts and guides us. I am deeply grateful that I had the opportunity to learn and practice the self-heal and healing techniques.

During the Pandemic, every day, I transfer energy healing to myself, to my family and to others. This brought us energy, light and joy, more balance for our body and mind. This is the foundation for us to connect with Cosmic energy, and expand our energy level for healing purposes.

When I was young, I liked to help my mother to take care of my younger brothers and sisters, for homework, keeping an eye on them for their safety, for bedtime . . . I was happy to help as daily life could be overwhelming for her with a family of seven children.

I grew up in a country in time of war. Daily life was blended with insecurity, risks, difficulties. My parents taught us to care about our health as much as we can. This would shape my life and prepare me for the future.

Many years later, while raising three small children, I had an opportunity to learn about Human & Cosmic Energy with a teacher in Spirituality. I discovered that we can harness Cosmic Energy and transfer it to our body to self-heal on energetical level. I found the subject fascinating, and I studied it as a priority, as I felt that there was so much to explore and learn about Universal truths and inner Human Potential.

At that time, I had chronic migraines, sometimes with very serious ones. My headaches were so intensely painful that I had to stay in a dark room with no light and complete silence.

After implementing Cosmic energy self-healing techniques, my migraines were gone entirely after a few weeks and since then—30 years—I have not had another migraine or even a light headache.

I healed myself every day, for a few minutes and could benefit quickly from my well-being overall. My energetic level had improved to reach a balanced state for my physical health and mental clarity.

I could create a stable balance and alignment of my Mind–Body–Spirit.

I found my inner voice and it felt familiar, almost like being home.

The quality of my life had changed.

I was more active, feeling happy with this new tool and opportunity to heal myself, my children, my family and others.

Imagine what the world could be if everyone was willing and able to pursue their "inner potential" with these techniques to connect every day with Cosmic energy and self-heal as a daily practice for preserving life quality.

Imagine that you can choose to be more responsible, with tools and processes of how to maintain and preserve health with simple techniques to create a more balanced health state.

Why healing with Cosmic Energy?

I intuitively believe there is a Higher power from the Cosmos as a Light energy source for all living creatures, behind everything material we created on planet Earth.

I learnt that the frequencies of cosmic rays are extraordinarily high and very independent of time and space. Cosmic rays are not affected by the communication waves of radio, television, telephone or wireless devices, and vice versa.

The speed of cosmic rays is believed to be faster than the speed of light waves because it's in the fourth-dimensional world, which is known as the world of Spiritual energy waves.

The following is an excerpt from an article by Brian Resnick:

"Cosmic rays are messengers from the broader universe, a reminder that we are part of it and a reminder that there is still a great deal of mystery out there.

. . . These rays were potentially propelled by forces from far beyond our solar system by forces no physicist understands. That's plainly awesome."

I immediately loved the subject of how Cosmic Energy could impact Human energy.

As my mind expanded, my views of the Universe, human life on Earth, human mind, human body, human spirit and all that is in it did too. I was spontaneously happy and excited to have these stimulating solutions for the good of the many!

Here is something interesting. I love to understand how humans and all living creatures are created from cosmic rays.

Robert Millikan addressed before the largest scientific society in America:

"Cosmic rays are the birth of atoms being born in interstellar space. They present the first experimental evidence that the Creator is still on the job . . ."

My mind and soul were now "open" to a much larger understanding of the Universe that had been awakened by something inside me. There is something logical, intelligent, well structured from the Cosmos that I can discover, research and develop through experiences.

Through the many years of practicing and implementing these self-heal techniques in daily life, for myself, for my family, friends and people around, I found I could simplify and structure everything into an easy 3-step process and system where I could share my expertise to people who choose to take action and embrace a new opportunity to not only taking care of themself but also help others, as a contribution to community and society.

While it was the most exciting time of my life, through learning, practicing, developing and doing a lot of self-exploration, my life was being guided step by step, as it was unfolding gradually and naturally.

I had the opportunity to teach and transfer my experiences in many different countries in Europe, Asia, Turkey, Israel, South Africa, South America, USA.

These are valuable experiences for me to grow, learn and be a part of some extraordinary contribution to society.

I was feeling that sharing these experiences is a responsibility and duty to transfer to anyone seeking improvement in these fundamental areas of their life, balancing their Mind–Body–Spirit energy.

After eight years of learning, practicing, teaching, through experiences, I received my Doctor of Philosophy certification (Ph. D.) in 1998 from *The Open International University for Complementary Medicines.*

In 2006, I was certified as a Hado Instructor, trained by Dr. Masaru Emoto, whose research has revealed how thoughts and words vibrate and interact within our subtle vibrational energies and impact our physical balance.

You may have heard of his work with water and the effects of sounds from words, music, creating positive or negative vibrations on water molecules that we can observe on water crystals as snow flakes,—when the water just started to freeze—that impact our health system.

Everything that I have learned, researched and practiced daily was realized step by step, and anyone who implements these simple yet efficient healing techniques can create their Mind–Body–Spirit Balance . . . in much less time than it took me.

By implementing my **Instant Balance** 3-step proven system, you can achieve the same results I've been able to achieve for myself. An immediate opportunity to embrace techniques to Self-heal Physical health, Mental clarity and have Spiritual Awakening.

STEP 1: COMMUNICATE

Working on Activation of the Energy centers of Transformation (Chakras in Sanskrit language) to harness Cosmic energy and Self-heal Techniques to transfer to yourself, healing others, balancing and restoring physical health on an energetic level.

Simple Breathing techniques to focus and communicate with your Inner potential to ignite alignment of body and mind, with more feelings of energy flow are the first steps to balance your physical health.

STEP 2: CLARIFY

Expanding your vibrational feelings of energy flow on chakras, implementing specific techniques of chakras spinning to develop your Intuition (6th sense) and perform Distant healing Techniques.

These techniques will support you to Clarify your thoughts and thinking with more focus and structure to ground yourself in real time, in the moment present and expand your Brilliance and Mind focus.

These specific techniques of working with your intuitive potential develop discernment of what is real and true from what is fake and illusion in life to continuously expand and elevate your consciousness.

STEP 3: CREATE

The third step is to empower you to Create in full consciousness—whatever you want to create, your thoughts and thinking, your choices, create your outcome, create a life by design and not by default.

You are the Creator of your life path, for yourself and others while you can continuously contribute through healing yourself, family and community.

We have so much to be grateful for, and I recognized that it was an opportunity to embrace, apply for myself and others.

Creativity is unlimited. You Create Harmony, Joy and Love through conscious living with deeper values, responsibilities and contribution.

The foundation is still to have tools to Self-heal your physical health, mental clarity daily and awaken your spiritual potential.

I have witnessed so many significant changes in the life of people who implement these techniques. Humans are created with many Inner potentials and Self-heal is one among many.

If you have the desire to be more aware of yourself, create a life to fulfill your purpose, then igniting self-healing potential is the first step for you to embrace, to awaken your spiritual being.

Energy healing can be applied anytime, anywhere.

You can maintain and preserve your health, tap into your inner potential and gradually discover your purpose in life on planet Earth.

As everything is constantly moving on energy level and evolving, I believe life is granted to humans to embrace the opportunity to discover, learn and experience to elevate our consciousness and co-create through our earthly life in contribution to our Earth and the Universe.

When experiencing our life on Earth with full consciousness, we are guided by the Light source and reflect our uplifted energy frequencies through our conscious living.

What if we have tools and techniques to experience and create?

I encourage you to tap into your Inner potential, wherever you may be on your path. You may be new in this field, you may already be conscious and practicing, or you are living it and sharing it with the world. I salute all of you and thank you for your awareness and your presence on Earth.

Thank you for reading my chapter in this book. I have a gift for you to practice as often as you feel it is needed: **Recharging Breathing technique**, a fundamental technique to practice at any time anywhere, to recharge and balance instantly your Mind–Body–Spirit:

- **Eyes open, breathe in calmly, and breathe out longer, softly.**
- **Repeat 3 times.**

Breathing in is to harness the energy from the Universe into your body, breathing out is to relieve preoccupations, anxieties, worries, fear, the four obstacles slowing us to grow on our spiritual path.

This simple technique has a greater impact on your health than you may think.

It helps you to be more grounded and be in the moment present, creating Instant Balance on your energy level.

If you can repeat this and create a new simple practice, a new habit in your life, you will notice a difference in your thinking and clarity, energy frequencies and in your well-being in general.

Start with a simple step and allow your potential to unfold.

As for everything, we apply techniques and structures as tools to experience growth and evolution on our path.

May your Inner Light shine out and be your guide!

May you create impacts to yourself, family and others.

With Love and Gratitude.
Minh H. Dannerstedt, PhD

Minh Dannerstedt, Ph D

Dr. Minh H. Dannerstedt started with Energy Self-healing Workshops in Europe and was invited to work in several countries on different continents, giving her opportunities to gain valuable experiences in coaching and mentoring.

She received a Certification of Doctor of Philosophy from the Open International University for Complementary Medicine in 1998 and is conducting workshops in English and French.

She is also a Certified Hado Instructor (Healing And Discovering Ourselves) guided by Dr. Masaru Emoto, whose researches have revealed through photographs of water crystals how Thoughts and Words interact with our vibrational subtle energies and physical balance.

Dr. Minh Dannerstedt is a Certified Coach in B.A.N.K. IOS (Intelligence Operating System) & Licensed Trainer in Personality Code for Sales, Communication & Relationships at Code Breaker Tech.

Dr. Minh Dannerstedt is now bringing her Instant Balance 3-step proven system on digital platforms to reach a larger audience and contribute with her life work.

Visit **https://Time2selfheal.com**
Email: **time2selfheal@gmail.com**

https://www.facebook.com/Minhh.Dann
Instagram: Minhd.hado
linkedin.com/in/wellnessexecutive

YOU DECIDE
BY KATHRYN SORAIZ

It happened last Saturday . . .

Pressure had been building. Everything seemed to go wrong that day. Weeks earlier, on Christmas Eve, my husband had walked out of our 32-year marriage. Were we fighting? No. He simply left and took nothing . . . absolutely nothing.

For many days, I didn't know what was going on. Was he alright? Where was he? Why had he gone?

And, even though I help people resolve sleep issues and made sure I got sufficient sleep, I barely functioned. In a daze, is it any wonder I lost my phone?

I was desperate to get to the Apple store at the mall. Doesn't sound like a dire need, does it? First world problem, right? Yet, in that moment, it all came to a head.

I'd already been to the AT&T store. After waiting over an hour for service, I was informed my replacement phone would arrive in 7 to 10 business days. What?! "Disrupted supply chain," the employee said.

I needed my phone for 2-factor verification of my email. My bank and credit card companies wouldn't talk to me to help sort out ownership and bills without sending a security code to the phone number in their records.

Clients made appointments and I was unaware . . . yeah, not my finest hour. My husband gone; my kids spread across the country. I felt so alone.

As I raced to the mall, I noticed a rare parking spot near the door. I quickly turned into the row of parked cars and . . . that's when it happened. I felt the right front tire jump the curb and heard the horrible scrape on the underside of the car. Then the car went down again. I'd wedged my car atop the triangular-shaped concrete endcap.

I exited to assess the damage, then returned to the car and tried to back up. More scraping ensued, followed by no movement at all. Zip, nada, nothing.

The mall would close in less than an hour and I was leaving town before dawn the next morning. I was ready to give up and leave the car where it was. As I got out, a kind man who had dropped his wife off at Macy's rolled down his window.

"Are you alright?" he asked. Now I was ready to cry.

Just then, a lady left Macy's, saw me by the car, and quickly made her way over. "That must have made a horrible noise. I'd be scared out of my mind," she said.

Suddenly, I didn't feel so vulnerable. The gentleman drove off and the lady stayed to talk a moment. I was grateful to both of them for their kindness and consideration. Life started to make sense, again.

Good thing it was 2022 rather than 2020! Would they have come over to help so early in the pandemic? Would we be conversing at all?

Pandemic Outcomes

In a lot of respects, the pandemic has been a shitshow. Heartache, loss, upset, financial hardship and fear loomed for many. I've spoken with hundreds of people. Surprisingly, the majority shared that remarkable good also resulted.

Many, like Angela Stoud, have an immediate response. "It allowed me to spend more time with my kids. We ate dinner together every night. We got to be close, again."

"My dad got [the virus] and died last year," said Imelda Castillo. "I miss him," she said as tears welled up in her eyes. "The gift that losing him gave to me was to honor time with my mother. Now I have dates with my mother. We really look after her and keep in touch with her. If it weren't for my father dying, I wouldn't be so intentional about being as close to her as I am."

By the end, she's smiling. They all do. No matter how many people I meet, at the end of their tale, there's a lightness, a warmth—a human connecting with me. Would we have spoken before? Probably not. We'd have been off in our own minds with our lists of things to do . . . too busy to notice one another.

Do you remember the early days of the pandemic? In line at a store, when someone coughed, did your ears perk up? Mine did.

I won't lie. Wearing masks was challenging for some . . . not me. I come from a family of germaphobes. My maternal grandmother Eugenia began having children around 1919. By 1921, my eldest aunt, Genoveva, was born. My grandmother had two children prior to my aunt's birth, both died in infancy. The first lived 7 months, the second a mere 3 weeks.

My grandmother was devastated. My aunt's birth was the answer to her prayers, it also ushered in the start of my grandmother's OCD.

During her pregnancy, my grandmother took classes from the American Red Cross. There she began her lifelong war against "microbios" [microbes].

Plenty of people wash their hands carefully, or wash dishes in a way that keeps spots from forming on glassware and utensils. That's fine . . . that's normal. The practices my grandmother engaged in did not fall within normal guidelines.

When we moved to Austin, Texas, my grandmother unexpectedly informed my mother that they—my maternal grandparents— were coming with us.

It was a treasured time in my life and I lived my grandmother's version of "normal" every day. I was nearly 7 when I first learned that boiling water would kill most microbios. Some microbios survived the boiling water she'd pour over dishes to disinfect them while they dried on the drainboard.

But that wasn't enough. The dishes would cool to room temperature and she'd then pour pitchers of ice-cold water over them. This practice was repeated after each and every meal. Every. Single. Day.

My grandmother's belief was that males were inherently dirty. Despite severe poverty, no hand towels were shared between genders and each child had their own bath towel and washcloth.

There was only one bathroom in the house. Parents used it first—it then would be cleaned. The girls would use it next and boys would use it last. Nine kids. After everyone was finished, the bathroom would be sanitized. This happened multiple times a day.

Fast forward to Austin, my grandfather would use the bathroom and my grandmother would go in immediately after to scrub the toilet inside and out. Scrub the sink . . . inside and out. Wipe down the mirror and quickly damp mop the floor with a mixture of Pine-o-Pine and hot water.

She'd also tear off the next four panels of toilet paper—in case he'd touched them—then set them atop the commode to use the next time she used the bathroom. I wasn't allowed to touch the suspect panels. According to my grandmother, I lacked immunity to my grandfather's microbios. To this day, I still pull off the first four panels of toilet paper in public bathrooms.

But I touch them with my hands, right? So why be wasteful? No, my grandmother, mother, and favorite aunt each taught me to take a paper towel into the bathroom stall and use it to remove the offending toilet paper. The paper towel would also be used to lock and unlock the door to the stall. For each use, the paper towel was folded a particular way, always revealing a fresh, clean surface.

A new paper towel would be used to turn on the faucet and hold the bar of soap under water to wash away the microbios of the last person. When I finished with the soap, I would do my civic duty and rinse the soap, wipe down the soap dish and gently position the pristine soap remnant atop a neatly folded paper towel so the next person would know a "clean" person had used it. Yes, I really believed all this.

Is that it? Not by a long shot. And why bring all this up?

PANDEMIC RELIEF

For me and others in my extended family, the pandemic was a relief. Don't get me wrong. It was horrific for many. Untold trauma befell family after family. The relief I speak of is that we *got* to wear masks and gloves.

Let me explain . . .

We'd often carry tissue to open doors, touch light switches and press elevator buttons when out of the house. No more. Nitrile gloves and a little spray bottle with isopropyl alcohol protected us. Yes, I like wearing gloves. Go ahead, make fun.

Back to feeling relief. All of a sudden, others were aware of microbios in the world. Even doctors, dentists and schools had microbios on their radar and were cleaning to rid us of the potentially nasty critters. RELIEF.

Wait, but what about all of the chemicals and sprays and dirty masks and plastics. Crazy, right?! Yeah, it is.

Medicos stressed the agency each individual has: use masks when in close proximity with those outside your bubble AND take responsibility for your own health.

Rather than keeping microbios away, I was challenged to keep myself healthy and fit. I believe those two schools of thought work best in combination—much like a team.

Once more, I felt relief. It wasn't because of steps others took or even the acceptance I experienced when wearing a mask and gloves in public, it was due to the empowerment I felt within me.

These days, it's conventional to hear our feelings attributed to what happens to us in life—in other words, our circumstance. Though it's commonly believed that our circumstances dictate our feelings, I strongly disagree.

Consider this: a circumstance is simply a fact. It's a neutral event that everyone present agrees took place. For instance, let's pretend that Rachel and George are talking. George tells Rachel that he thinks her mother, Irene, is meddlesome.

A description of that circumstance would be: George said he thinks Irene is meddlesome.

Is what George says about Irene true? That's not relevant.

WHAAAAT?!

"But you didn't hear what that person said!" You're right. I didn't. Attributing a direct quote to the person who spoke it is merely a fact. Facts are neutral events.

"No, but s/he was rude and insulting and it hurt my feelings." Really? Let's look deeper.

C, T, F, A, R to The Rescue

Here's a radical concept: Other people's words don't cause us to feel a particular way. Our *thoughts* about the words the other person spoke are what actually generate our feelings.

Here's how it works . . .

Our brain is a sophisticated computer-ish component within us. It sorts out complex tasks and quickly creates a system for dealing with that situation so it doesn't have to repeat the effort, again.

For example: We learned to walk. Prior to walking, we figured out how to stand, find our balance, get one foot off the ground—put it somewhere—and then do the same with the other foot. If you've ever seen a baby practice, you know it takes time to perfect the process.

You probably walk with ease now; your brain has worked out the mechanics. Unless you break or strain something, you likely haven't thought about how to walk for quite some time. Your brain has systemized walking to a largely unconscious function.

That's how feelings work, too.

Feelings are learned. When we were young, we didn't know how we felt. Slowly but surely, we associated a thought about an event and its relation to us. That thought then generates a feeling.

When a feeling was generated as a result of a thought, we took action. That action could be anything: a frown, a smile, tears, overeating, running away, screaming, arguing . . .

And, because our computer-ish brain is so fabulously efficient, it decides, "Okay, I don't need to keep processing and analyzing this situation (the Circumstance) anymore. I know what needs to be done. Every time someone tells me, 'I hate you', I'll activate the 'hurt' feeling." Consider the C,T,F,A,R, example below:

Circumstance: Person A said, "I hate you."

Thought: You don't know me.

Feeling: Hurt

Action: sulk, cry, shrink, tell myself that I'm less than / inferior, I stay away from Person A

Result: I avoid Person A and keep Person A from knowing me.

Of course, the thought could have gone in another direction:

Circumstance: Person A said, "I hate you."

Thought: Go to hell!

Feeling: Angry

Action: yell, argue, body tightens, heart pounds, slam fists on the table, stomp off, leave

Result: I am done dealing with Person A and am ready to walk away.

We don't generally recognize all the processing that takes place. Mandates to wear masks outraged many. It was not the order itself that created the upset. Ensuing thoughts *about* the order provoked the feelings. Whether we acknowledge it or not, we each have agency in our lives.

The thoughts of others don't *make* us feel a particular way. We don't have that power over others, and others don't have that power over us.

Some people, like Leonard "Leo" Rico, already know this. The pandemic virus claimed the lives of his grandfather and uncle. As he put it, "I could have shut down and stopped when that happened. But my grandfather, my mother, and stepfather all taught me that whatever happens is up to me."

"Yeah, I was sad to lose my grandfather. I lived 11 years with him and I couldn't even go to his funeral. That was really hard. My work shut down for three weeks. I took one week off as a vacation and then I got another job. I've worked consistently through the pandemic. Mostly, [the pandemic] hasn't affected me," he continued.

"A few years ago, my mother and I began investing. That investment pays out quarterly. It pays me enough to cover all my bills. I live simply, and drive an older Honda. I'd like a Toyota, but my car takes me anywhere I want to go.

"I love to travel internationally. Other countries didn't let Americans in, so my fiancée and I began exploring our own back yard. We have a dream. She and I are on course to save enough that we can quit our jobs in two years. I've started a YouTube channel that I plan to monetize. It's slow going and, if it doesn't work, I can always come back and work for someone else. I'm only 32," Leo said, a large smile beaming across his face.

What does Leo do? He is waitstaff at a local IHOP.

Contrast Leo's attitude with my own that Saturday. I reacted and was human. The kind gentleman parked, then walked up to my car and offered to get it off the endcap. He got inside and, in short order, freed my vehicle.

The lady beside me wrapped her arm around my shoulders and softly said, "You and your car were always okay. You were just too scared to see what needed to be done."

Tilting her head over towards the kindly gentleman, she smiled and continued, "He wasn't afraid."

Now, neither am I.

What the pandemic has offered me is the awareness that everything is an opportunity to choose our response. What choice will you make?

Kathryn Soraiz

Sleep and eating go hand in hand...every one of us does both. Not all of us do them well.

Sleep dysregulation and digestive disorders combine to hundreds of billion-dollar industries. Are you still struggling?

In 2021, Kathryn Soraiz — The Sleep Sage™ and author of the book *Revenge: Sleep Procrastination*—founded an international practice devoted to elevating her clients' quality of life through improved sleep and metabolic function.

Kathryn became aware of her own sleep dysfunction in 2017. It resulted from more than a decade of childhood trauma. Realizing the centrality of sleep, she's made it her mission to reconnect people with their own Deep Sleeper Within™.

In 2022, Kathryn added YOH.Life's *Metabolic Reset* to address the synergetic nature of eating and sleeping. Kathryn's findings are the basis of her 90-day, money back guarantee, training: *Be the Sleep Sage in Your Own Life*™. This has resulted in deeper, more refreshing sleep, enhanced relationships, restored focus, and/or enriched quality of life for scores of her clients.

Look inside for the QR code and receive "20 Ways to Sleep Better."

SOCIAL MEDIA LINKS
Email: **TheTeam@YOH.Life**
Website: **YOH.Life**

CLOSING THOUGHTS

Dear Amazing Reader,

I hope you enjoyed reading these stories and were touched by these powerful chapters. Each author carefully hand-picked stories from their lives so they could inspire, educate and empower you to realize your brilliance—to give you a sense of hope and encouragement and let you know you are not alone and you can conquer any challenges that come your way. You got this!

We can't wait for you to become or expand into your true authentic self, to embrace your uniqueness and be the exceptional leader that you are. Celebrate as you share your heartfelt love and compassion with the world while practicing self-compassion and self-love.

I would like to share additional resources that will help you get unstuck and give you the tools that may be support you as you uplevel your life.

I offer several workshops, group programs and personal coaching.

1. **Other Books and My first anthology,** *The Authorities,* **with** *New York Times* **best-selling author, Dr. John Gray, from the** *Mars/Venus* **series.** My chapter is called "Break Free From Your Pain Cycle," in which I chronicle my transformation from being bedridden and in chronic pain to becoming a successful entrepreneur. I share the exact steps that I took that you can adopt for yourself. It's available on amazon

2. **Book Writing Opportunity**

Writing a book is an amazing way to share your expertise, knowledge and experiences. It gives an opportunity for your clients, prospects and your network to get to know you and build your influence.

It is also an incredible way to Increase Your **Visibility** where you are seen as an **Expert, Expand Your Influence,** and **Make a Global Impact as a Published Author!**

Whether you are an established author or aspiring writer, our programs will support you. It is our goal to take the pressure off of the entire publishing work for you to become a published author so that you can focus on your writing to reach the readers who are yearning to hear your informative and life-changing message, and to boost your visibility, influence, and success.

We are providing a platform for the everyday heroes in our backyards to share their amazing stories and become known, seen and heard. Yes! You too can be a published author! Usually, the first thought that comes in everybody's mind is that "I don't have a story." Believe us, you do! We all have a story; to find yours, you can schedule a complimentary discovery call here: **http://bit.ly/TalkwithSeema**

3. **High Performance Coaching**

I support leaders to fully step into the power of self-leadership, to become powerful change agents who lead themselves authentically—shifting limiting beliefs and patterns of behavior to create more fulfilling experience. Authentic leadership cultivates meaningful connection that helps everyone thrive.

4. **Reboot Wellness Program**

It is important to stay on top of your game. That is taking care of your body so that you can focus on getting the results you want. That is why I have a created a 16-week program for women entrepreneurs and leaders to learn how they can eat, move and think differently as a key to ultimately create a life by your design, no longer by default.

You will learn:

- 4 Pillars to a healthier lifestyle
- Learn to make better life choice
- Reclaim your body, mind and spirit to live in the flow of your passion by building a strong wellness foundation.

5. *Break Free to Brilliance Podcast.* Tune in to hear heart-centered guests for inspiration and insight as they share their experiences on how they broke free from their life challenges to live their purpose-driven life. These are the everyday heroes that you find in your backyard—mothers, sisters, friends, entrepreneurs and business owners. We bring positive and transformational messages to the world so that we can make a lasting difference and help individuals powerfully live purposefully, one show at a time. You can tune in **here** or your favorite podcast listening place.

6. Meditation Mastermind

Master Your Inner Game is all about self-care and performance mastery

It is designed to help you create a deeper connection with your inner and outer world where you feel you are one in all dimensions of your life.

You will gain:

- Clarity that will Increase Focus
- Increased energy
- Inner peace, love, joy and balance
- Fear and Frustration to Confident and Stand in Your Power
- Overwhelm to Alignment with your Mind, Body & Soul
- Build stronger Immune System
- Belief that Self Care is Selfless

And so much more . . .

7. We are continuously coming up with new, free resources to help you navigate how you want to move forward. You can find them at www. uplyft.media

8. One of the key catalysts in turning my health around has been whole food supplements and the tower garden growing my own food. You can find more information at **www.seema.juiceplus.com**

If you are ready to shine and share your story of breaking free from challenges and living life on your terms, and if you are ready to help others stand in their power, you can participate in our upcoming anthologies and podcast.

If you would like to personally connect with me to explore opportunities in my programs, podcasts and book writing projects, then schedule a time with me at **http://bit.ly/TalkwithSeema**, or you can email me at **seema@ seemagiri.com**

May you always STAND IN YOUR POWER!

Sincerely,

"There are two primary choices in life: to accept conditions as they exist, or accept the responsibility for changing them."
—Dennis Waitley

What choices are you making?